The WAY *of* PRAYER

TERESA *of* AVILA

The WAY *of* PRAYER

LEARNING TO PRAY WITH THE OUR FATHER

Edited and translated by William J. Doheny, C.S.C.

Christian Classics *Notre Dame, Indiana*

Founded in 1865, Ave Maria Press is a ministry of the Indiana Province of Holy Cross.

www.christian-classics.com

ISBN-10 0-87061-246-8 ISBN-13 978-0-87061-246-6

Cover and text design by Brian C. Conley.

Printed and bound in the United States of America.

Library of Congress Cataloging-in-Publication Data

Teresa, of Avila, Saint, 1515-1582.

The way of prayer : learning to pray with the Our Father / Teresa of Avila ; adapted by William J. Doheny.

p. cm.

"This edition consists mainly of Teresa's commentary on the Lord's Prayer which comprised the last sixteen chapters of The way of perfection. An introductory section contains her teaching on the practice of vocal and mental prayer, drawn from chapters 22/26 of the source. Fr. Doheny's translation, which employed archaic English, has been updated and adapted for this edition"--Editor's note.

ISBN-13: 978-0-87061-246-6

ISBN-10: 0-87061-246-8

1. Lord's prayer--Early works to 1800. I. Doheny, William J. (William Joseph), 1898- II. Teresa, of Avila, Saint, 1515-1582. Way of perfection. III. Title.

BV230.T43 2008

226.9'606--dc22

2007046584

CONTENTS

EDITOR'S NOTE

The title of this book, *The Way of Prayer*, is adapted from the title of St. Teresa of Avila's longer work *The Way of Perfection* from which this volume has been excerpted. *The Way of Perfection* was composed as a guide to prayer and the religious life for the members of Teresa's order of Carmelite sisters in sixteenth-century Spain. It is considered Teresa's most accessible work and continues to speak to readers today in all walks of life. In the first half of her book, Teresa speaks to the nuns about the virtues necessary for religious life: mutual love, detachment from self and the world, and humility. In the second half, Teresa instructs them on the practice of vocal and mental prayer and meditates on individual sections of the Lord's Prayer. "The way of prayer" is a phrase that Teresa uses frequently in her commentary, encouraging her sisters to grow in "the way of prayer" and remain faithful to it.

This current edition has its origin in Holy Cross Father William J. Doheny's book *The Pater Noster of Saint Teresa* published in 1942 by The Bruce Publishing Company. This book is one of many classic spiritual works that he translated and edited in an effort to make the works of the mystics known and available at a time when they were not so widely distributed as today. He personally published and freely distributed many of these books to religious and lay readers alike to foster the knowledge and practice of prayer. During his lifetime Fr. Doheny served in numerous ministries. He was Dean of the Notre Dame Law School, Assistant Superior of the Congregation of Holy Cross, and Advocate and Procurator of the Roman Rota. He died in 1982.

This edition consists mainly of Teresa's commentary on the Lord's Prayer which comprised the last sixteen chapters of *The Way of Perfection.* An introductory section contains her teaching on the practice of vocal and mental prayer, drawn from chapters 22–26 of the source. Fr. Doheny's translation, which employed archaic English, has been updated and adapted for this edition.

We have sought to honor his legacy by remaining faithful to the intention he expressed in the introduction to his work:

Wherever this commentary of the saint has been read and meditated upon, it has invariably proved helpful to souls. The aim of the present edition is to bring the inexhaustible riches of this work of the incomparable Carmelite nun to laics as well as to priests, seminarians, Religious, and novices. Thus it is hoped that the twofold aim will be realized which the Church has embodied in the Oration for the Mass of the Saint; "May we be nourished with the food of her heavenly teaching, and by our desire of loving devotedness, may we grow in knowledge of you."

INTRODUCTION

As is well known, the chapters in this book constitute the concluding part of a larger work of St. Teresa titled The Way of Perfection. *It has been thought advisable to include here a few points treated by her elsewhere in the complete work. These additional thoughts are intended to serve as an introduction to provide for the better understanding of the saint's commentary on the Our Father.*

Oh Absolute Sovereign of the world! You are Supreme Omnipotence, Sovereign Goodness, Wisdom itself! You are without beginning and without end. Your works are limitless, your perfections infinite, and your intelligence is supreme! You are a fathomless abyss of marvels! Oh Beauty, containing all other beauty! Oh great God, you are Strength itself! Would that I possessed at this moment all the combined eloquence and wisdom of men! Then, in so far as it is possible here below, where knowledge is so limited, I could strive to make known one of your innumerable perfections. The contemplation of these reveals to some extent the nature of him who is our Lord and our only Good.

Mental Prayer

My dear sisters, draw close to him; but realize and understand to whom you are about to speak or whom you are already addressing. Even after a thousand lives like our own, you would never understand how to act with this Lord, before whom the angels tremble. He rules the entire universe. He can do all. For him, to will is to accomplish. . . .

To understand these truths well is to practice mental prayer. If you wish to combine vocal prayer with this, that is perfectly suitable. But when you speak to God, do not direct your attention to other things. To do so would be to fail to understand mental prayer. . . . If one wishes to pray perfectly, one must strive wholeheartedly to be recollected.

Resolute Determination in Prayer

. . . I reiterate that it is very important to enter upon this way of prayer with the resolute determination to persevere in it. . . . Since we wish to devote to God certain times of prayer, let us give these to him with a spirit that is generous and untrammeled with earthly thoughts. Let us give this time with the firm resolution never to take it back, no matter what trials, contradictions, or aridities may come. Reckon this time as something no longer belonging to us, but time for which we shall be held accountable on the score of justice, if we do not dedicate ourselves entirely to it. . . . God is ever attentive in order to repay us for our services to him. Do not fear that he will ever permit the least action to go unrewarded, even one so insignificant as the lifting of your eyes to heaven, in remembrance of him.

Satan's Fear of Valiant Souls

The second reason why we should resolutely devote ourselves to prayer is that Satan thereby has less chance to tempt us. He is most fearful of valiant souls. He knows from experience what harm they cause him. Everything Satan does to injure valiant souls profits them and their neighbor, and he comes away from the combat as the loser. Nevertheless, we ought not be negligent nor become less cautious. We must strive against traitors. If we are vigilant, they will not have the courage to attack us, because they are cowards. But if they notice that we are no longer alert, they can inflict great harm on us. As soon as they detect that a soul is vacillating, inconstant, and not resolutely determined to persevere, they will torment it day and night without ceasing. They will suggest a thousand fears and conjure up endless difficulties. Experience has taught me this at great cost, and that is why I speak of it to you. And I add that no one can possibly appreciate fully how important this counsel is.

Heroic Courage of Resolute Persons

The third very important reason for determined devotedness to prayer is that a resolute person fights with greater courage. He then realizes that he must never retreat, no matter what the odds may be. Notice the soldier on the battlefield. He knows that if he loses, his life is at stake, and that if he does not die in the thick of the battle, he will be executed afterward. And thus he fights more unflinchingly and is determined to sell his life dearly, as the saying goes. He has no fear of wounds because he is intent upon gaining the victory, and he realizes that victory is the only means of saving his life.

Assurance of Success in Prayer

Furthermore, it is necessary to begin with the assurance that we shall succeed, unless we deliberately permit ourselves to be vanquished. Success is absolutely certain. No matter how insignificant our gain may be, it will enrich us immeasurably. As I have previously stated and would like to repeat a thousand times, do not fear that our Lord will permit you to die of thirst after having invited you to drink of this fountain. Fear paralyzes to a great extent the ardor of those persons who have never had personal experience of our Lord's goodness, even though their faith assures them of it. I assure you that it is a great advantage to have known his friendship and to have experienced the tender care he bestows upon those who follow this way of prayer. . . .

Vocal Prayer

My dear sisters, again I address myself to those souls who can neither recollect themselves nor concentrate their minds in mental prayer, nor can they make a meditation. We must avoid the very mention of these words, for persons of that type are not interested in such things. In fact, there are many who seem to be frightened by the very term *mental prayer* or *contemplation*. . . .

I shall teach you how you ought to pray vocally. It is only right that you should understand what you say. Perhaps those who are incapable of centering their thoughts on God will likewise become wearied by long prayers. I shall not treat of long prayers, but only of those every Christian is obliged to recite, namely, the Our Father, and the Hail Mary.

Proper Recitation of Vocal Prayers

When I recite the Creed, it seems only reasonable that I should advert to and understand what I believe. Likewise, when I recite the Our Father, it would be a mark of love to recall who this Father is, and who the Master is who taught us this prayer. If you should reply that it suffices to reflect upon this Master just once and for all, you might as well argue that it is sufficient to recite this prayer once in a lifetime. . . .

May God grant that we should be not unmindful of him when we recite this prayer. However, it sometimes happens that we do forget him, because of our frailty. . . . I have already stated that one cannot speak to God and to the world at the same time. Still, this is exactly what those do who recite their prayers while listening to the conversation of others, or who dwell on other thoughts without any effort to banish distractions. . . .

Solitude During Prayer

We should strive to seek solitude during prayer, in so far as we are able. And God grant that this may suffice to make us realize both the presence of him who is with us and the answer that our Lord makes to our petitions. Do you think that he is silent, even though we cannot hear him? Assuredly not! He speaks to the heart when the heart entreats him.

Close Union With Jesus

It would be well for us to consider that our Lord has taught this prayer to each one of us, individually, and that he still teaches it to us at this very moment. The Master is never so distant that his disciple need raise his voice to be heard. On the contrary, he is very near. To enable you to recite the Our Father well, I should like to see you perfectly convinced of this truth, namely, that you must remain close to the Master who teaches it to you.

Relationship Between Vocal and Mental Prayer

You may again object that to pray thus would be meditation, and that you cannot, and consequently will not, pray except vocally. . . . I admit that you are right in calling this method mental prayer. But at the same time, I assure you that I do not understand how vocal prayer, when well-recited, can possibly be separated from mental prayer. We ought to realize to whom we are speaking. In fact, it is a duty to devote oneself with attention to prayer. God grant that all these means may aid us in reciting the Our Father well, and that we do not finish it amidst distracting thoughts! From experience, I have discovered that the best remedy against distractions is to strive to concentrate my thoughts on him to whom I address my prayers. Be patient, then, and strive to become habituated to this method, which is so necessary. It is indispensable for the formation of real religious and, if I am not mistaken, even for the proper recitation of the prayers of true Christians.

Distinction Between Vocal Prayer, Mental Prayer, and Contemplation

Contemplation

Do not mistakenly believe that one draws only little profit from vocal prayer when it is well made. I assure you that it is quite possible for our Lord to raise you to perfect contemplation while you are reciting the Our Father or some other vocal prayer. And thus his Majesty shows that he hears one who prays in such a manner. This Sovereign Master speaks to the soul in return, suspends its understanding, checks its thoughts and, as it were, forms the very words before they are pronounced. And thus of oneself one cannot utter a single word without the greatest effort. The soul then realizes that the Master teaches it without any sound of words. He suspends the activity of the faculties which, instead of gaining benefits, would only cause harm if they tried to act.

In this state, the faculties are filled with delight without knowing how they rejoice. The soul is inflamed with an increasing flow of love without perceiving how it loves. It knows that it enjoys the object of its love, but does not comprehend the nature of this enjoyment. Nevertheless, it realizes that the understanding of itself could never yearn for so ineffable a good. It realizes, too, that the will embraces the good without the soul's knowing how the will does this. If the soul can comprehend anything at all, its comprehension consists in the realization of the fact that nothing in the world could possibly merit this benefit. It is a gift of the Master of heaven and earth, who in the end bestows this gift in a manner worthy of him. This is contemplation. You can now understand wherein it differs from mental prayer.

Simplicity of Mental Prayer

Mental prayer, I repeat, consists in pondering over and seeking to understand what we say, in realizing to whom we speak, and who we are that we presume to address his Sovereign Majesty. To be preoccupied with these and similar considerations, such as the realization of the little we do for the service of God and of the obligation we are under to serve him, is to make mental prayer. Therefore, do not imagine that it involves some very hidden mystery and do not be frightened by the term *mental prayer.*

To recite the Our Father, the Hail Mary, or any other prayer of your choice is vocal prayer. But realize how discordant it would be without mental prayer. The very words do not otherwise follow in proper sequence. In contemplation, which I just described, we can do nothing of ourselves. His Majesty does everything therein. It is his work, and it transcends the powers of our nature. . . . He alone can bestow upon you the gift of contemplation. He will not refuse it if you do not loiter on the way, and if you do not neglect anything necessary to reach your destination.

The Need for Recollection

Let us return now to the consideration of vocal prayer. We should recite vocal prayers in such a way that we may receive all the other kinds of prayer as well from God. But to pray properly, you know that you must at the outset examine your conscience, recite the Confiteor and make the Sign of the Cross. Immediately after, seek companionship, and how could you possibly do better than to seek the company of the Master himself, who taught you the prayer you are to recite?

Method During Prayer

Picture our Lord near you. Consider the love and the humility with which he instructs you. Believe me, you ought to strive always to be ever near so faithful a Friend. If you accustom yourselves to consider him near you, and he sees you doing this with love, and striving to please him, you will be unable, so to speak, to dismiss him. He will never fail you. He will aid you in all your trials, and you will constantly be in his company. Do you think it an unimportant thing to have such a Friend near you?

The Need for Recollection

You who cannot develop thoughts with understanding nor fix your attention on a sacred mystery without distractions, accustom yourselves to this practice that I point out to you. I know that you can do it. During many years, I myself suffered from my inability to concentrate on any subject during prayer. And this is a terrible trial. Nevertheless, I know that our Lord never abandons us so completely as to refuse us his company if we humbly entreat him. If we do not acquire this favor within a year, let us strive several years for it. Do not begrudge time so well spent. And who is there to hurry us? You can, I repeat, accustom yourselves to this practice. Strive to remain in the company of this true Master.

Simple Gazing on Jesus

I am not asking you at this time to fix your attention on him, nor to engage in discursive reasoning, nor to make subtle and learned considerations. All that I request is that you direct the glance of your soul to him. Who is there who can prevent the turning of your gaze toward our Lord, even if only for a moment? Is it conceivable that you can look upon the most hideous things and still not have the power to behold the most ineffable sight imaginable? If you do not find him beautiful, you need never look upon him again. He, however, looks upon you constantly. Although you have offended him by a thousand insults and indignities, he has been patient with you. Despite your faults, he has never ceased to fix his gaze upon you. Is it too much, then, to ask that you withdraw your gaze from exterior things to contemplate him sometimes? . . . He values your glance so highly that he will neglect no means to ingratiate himself with you.

Loving Study of Jesus

. . . Our Lord condescends to be subject to you, and wishes you to act as sovereign. He submits himself to your will. Are you joyful? Contemplate him then in his resurrection. You have nothing else to do but to think of the glory with which he rose from the sepulcher, and you will be filled with joy. What splendor, what beauty, what majesty, what glory, and what exultation in his triumph! How gloriously he comes forth from the field of battle where he won so great a kingdom, which is destined entirely for you. And at the same time, he gives himself to you with this kingdom. Is it, then, too much for you to raise your eyes occasionally toward this Master who has bestowed such bountiful gifts upon you?

Jesus in His Person

Are you pensive or sad? Behold your Lord then as he goes to the Garden of Olives. What overwhelming affliction fills his soul! He who is patience itself manifests and avows his sufferings! Or look upon him bound to the column, covered with wounds and his flesh torn to shreds. And this is the measure of his great love for you! In the midst of his anguish, see how he is cruelly treated by some, spat upon by others, denied and deserted by his friends without a single person to plead his cause. He is stiff from the cold and so extremely lonely that he and you may well console each other.

Jesus, the Divine Model

Or, behold him bearing the cross, and not even given time to breathe. He will then turn to you with his beautiful and compassionate eyes filled with tears. He will even forget his sufferings to console you in yours, solely because you sought consolation from him and turned your gaze upon him. . . .

Observe the insupportable weariness that weighs upon him and realize how his sufferings surpass yours. No matter how great you may imagine your trials to be, and however painful they may appear, you will gain confidence in reflecting that they are but trifles compared with the sufferings of our Lord.

Perhaps you will say: if we had seen his Majesty with our bodily eyes when he lived on earth, we would follow your advice wholeheartedly, and we would fix our gaze upon him constantly. But I say: do not be deluded. Whoever does not make an effort now to behold our Lord within his soul, when this entails no great danger or sacrifice, he assuredly would not have been at the foot of the cross with Magdalene when the risk of death was involved.

Who can describe the sufferings of the glorious Virgin and this holy saint? . . . Indeed, their ordeal of suffering must have been terrible. Nevertheless, they were oblivious to their own sufferings because they personally beheld a spectacle of suffering more poignant by far than their own. So then, do not deceive yourselves into believing that you could have borne such trials if you cannot conquer the slight difficulties I mentioned. Perfect yourselves first of all in the small things so as to become capable of greater deeds.

Union With God

Again, I assure you that if you resolutely practice this method, you will reap benefits so great that it is really impossible for me to describe them. Therefore, remain close to this good Master. Keep the firm resolution to learn all that he teaches you. His Majesty will then see to it that you become his faithful disciples. This great God will never leave you unless you first abandon him. Meditate on the words that come from the divine lips. At the very outset, you will understand the love he has for you. And it is no small favor nor negligible joy for a disciple to see that he is loved by his Master.

CHAPTER ONE

"OUR FATHER, WHO ART IN HEAVEN"

The Father and the Son

Oh my God, how fitting it is that you are the Father of such a Son. And how well he proves himself the Son of such a Father. Be blessed forever! Would it not have been sufficient, oh Lord, if we had been permitted to address you thus at the *end* of this prayer? But it is at the very outset that you fill our hands and grant us so great a favor. Its remembrance should so fill our minds and inflame our wills that we become powerless to utter a single word. Here indeed, oh devoted souls of Christ, would be the proper place to discourse upon perfect contemplation!

Oh how profitably might the soul withdraw into itself! It would then be better able to rise above itself and to reflect upon what this holy Son would teach it about the heavenly abode of the Father. Let us leave this world. It is not fitting that we who have once realized the value of such a favor, should underestimate it by letting our thoughts remain on earth.

Christ, Our Brother

Oh Son of God and my Lord! How is it that you give us so much to think about with the very first word? You so humble yourself as to unite yourself with us in our petitions, and to make yourself the brother of creatures so vile and miserable as we are! How is it that in the name of the Father you give us all that can be given? Is it not that you wish him to regard us as his children? Since your desire cannot go unheeded, you oblige him to fulfill it; and that is no small task. Because he is our Father, he must bear with us, despite the gravity of our offenses. He must pardon us when, like the prodigal son, we return to him. He must console us in our trials. He must care for us in a manner becoming a divine Father. Since he possesses all perfections, he will of necessity be a better Father than all earthly fathers. And in addition to all this, he must make us partakers of his riches and coheirs with you.

The Love of Jesus for Us

Consider, oh my Lord, that you do not shrink from any obstacle, so great is your wonderful love for us, and so profound your humility. But since, oh Lord, in assuming our nature, you descended to earth and were clothed in our human flesh, it seems fitting that you should watch over our welfare. But consider that your Father is in heaven ; you yourself tell us so. It is only right, then, that even though you offered yourself to suffer shame for love of us, you give some thought to your Father's honor, and thus leave him free. Oblige him not to lavish so many favors upon a creature as vile and ungrateful as I am. And, oh good Jesus, how manifestly you show that you are but one with him and that your will is his and his is yours. What a striking proof of the great love you bear us!

Whereas from the demon you deliberately concealed the fact that you are the Son of God, yet out of your ardent desire for our good, you surmount every obstacle in order to make us understand this sublime truth. And who but you, oh Lord, could so enlighten us? I do not understand how Satan in hearing this word, "Father," did not unmistakably recognize who you are. But this at least I see clearly, oh my Jesus, that you spoke as a beloved Son, both for yourself and for us. And what is more, you are all powerful to accomplish in heaven whatever you said on earth. Blessed be you forever, oh my Lord! Your happiness consists in bestowing your gifts, and nothing can stay your loving generosity.

Attention to the Meaning of Words

And now, oh devoted souls of Christ, does he not appear to you a kind Master, who, in order to lead us to learn his teachings, begins by bestowing on us so marked a favor? Is it not fitting that when your lips pronounce these words, "Our Father," you should fix your attention on their meaning and allow your heart to express its gratitude at the thought of such love?

What son is there in this world who does not strive to know intimately a father whom he sees to be good, dignified, and powerful? Were he unable to find these qualities in him, I am certain that he would be unwilling to be known as his son. The world, moreover, is such that the son, if he be in a position superior to his father's, considers himself dishonored in acknowledging any relationship. This is not our case here. May it please God that such sentiments never exist in this house. That condition would be a veritable hell. On the contrary, let her who belongs to the most noble family seldom speak of her father, for you must live in perfect equality.

A Life of Perfect Equality

Oh college of the apostles formed by Christ! Tough St. Peter was only a fisherman, but the Lord conferred more authority on him than on St. Bartholomew, who was reputedly the son of a king. His Majesty well knew what endless disputes there would be in this world over the claims of birth. But is this not like arguing about what kind of clay is better suited for bricks than for an earthen wall? Oh my God, what an insignificant trifle! May God deliver you, oh souls devoted to Christ, from engaging in such contentions, even though it be only in jest. I trust that his Majesty will grant you this grace. But should any one of you fail even a little on this point, the abuse must be checked immediately. And let the religious fear lest she be as a Judas among the apostles. Let a penance be imposed on her until she thoroughly understands that she is not fit to be even common clay.

What a good Father the kind Jesus gives you! Let no other Father be known here, for with him alone you should be concerned. Strive ever to find your joy in him, and to confide yourselves entirely to his care. You know full well that if you remain faithful children, he will never abandon you. And who of us would not strive to avoid losing such a Father. Oh, what an admirable source of consolation are these thoughts!

But lest my comments be too lengthy, I leave you now to your own reflections. No matter how wandering your thoughts may be, keep yourselves in the presence of this Father and the Son, and you will, of necessity, find the Holy Spirit. May he inflame your hearts! May he forcibly unite them to himself with the all powerful bonds of his charity, if self-interest does not prompt you to do so.

CHAPTER TWO

"WHO ART IN HEAVEN" *(continued)*

God Within the Soul

Consider, now, this word of your Master, "Who art in heaven." Do you think it of little importance to know what heaven is and where it is you must seek your adorable Father? I assure you that it is very important for restless intellects not only to believe this truth, but to endeavor to realize it by experience; for such a realization is a very great aid to concentration of mind and to recollection of soul.

You know that God is everywhere. Now, it is clear that where a king dwells, there is his court. Heaven then, is where God dwells. Consequently, you can believe most surely that wherever his Majesty is, there also is all his glory.

Recall the words of St. Augustine, in which he says that after seeking God in many places, he found him within himself. Do you consider it a small favor that a soul accustomed to be easily distracted, should understand this truth and know that to speak to the Eternal Father, and to enjoy the blessings of his company, it does not have to ascend to heaven? No, the soul has no need to raise its voice to speak to him, who is so near that he hears all, even the faintest word. And of what use are wings in seeking him? It is enough that the soul find solitude and there behold him within itself. Nor should it wonder at the exceeding goodness of the divine Guest! But let the soul humble itself profoundly and address and beseech him as a Father. Without forgetting its unworthiness to be his creature, let the soul make known its trials and ask him for help.

The Danger of False Reticence

Put aside the excessive reticence into which certain persons fall, and who mistake this for humility! Humility does not consist in refusing a favor from a king, but rather in accepting and enjoying it with a gratitude that springs from the sense of our unworthiness. Assuredly, it would be a strange sort of humility that, when the Sovereign of heaven and earth would come to lavish his favors upon me and to rejoice with me, would forbid my answering him, or remaining with him, or accepting his gifts, but that would rather urge me to go away and leave him alone! When he invites and even entreats me to present my petitions to him, I mistakenly believe that I prove my humility by remaining in my lonely helplessness!

The truth is that by thus refusing his gifts, I oblige him to depart. Put aside, oh devoted souls of Christ, such false humility. Treat with him as with a Father, a Brother, a Master, or as a divine Guest. Consider him now in one way, now in another. He himself will teach you what to do to please him. But do not be so senseless as to neglect to petition him for something. Remind him that he is your divine Friend, and that in word and deed, he should ever act toward you as such. Realize how very important it is to understand well this truth, that since God dwells within us, we ought to strive to remain there in his company.

The Prayer of Recollection

Even though it be vocal, this form of prayer helps the understanding to attain recollection much more quickly than any other form, and it is productive of most precious results. It is called the prayer of recollection because in it the soul brings together all its faculties and enters into itself to be with God. And thus, more quickly than by any other means, the divine

Master instructs the soul and bestows upon it the prayer of quiet. Consequently, the soul, so interiorly recollected, can meditate on the passion, can call God the Son to be present to itself and offer him to the heavenly Father without stirring the mind by going to seek him on the mount of Calvary, or in the garden or at the column.

Those among you who are able thus to enclose themselves in the little heaven of their soul where the Creator of heaven and earth dwells, and who can form the habit of excluding exterior things and of fleeing the occasions of distractions from without, can rest assured that they are following an excellent way, and that they will certainly come to drink at the very fountain of living water. By this way, they will journey far in a short time, just as the traveler aboard a ship propelled by a favorable wind arrives at his destination within a few days; whereas had he gone by land, his trip would have been very much longer. And this way is the heavenly road. I call it the way to heaven, for souls who travel it find themselves in the palace of the King. They are no longer on earth.

These souls may be said to have already put out to sea. Although they may not have completely departed the earth, nevertheless they at least do their best to free themselves from it by interior recollection. When this recollection is genuine, it is clearly discernible by a definite effect it produces. I do not know how to make you understand this, but those who have experienced it will understand. Perhaps one might put it this way, that the soul, now that it has finally perceived the things of this world to be nothing but worthless trifles, rises at the most convenient moment and departs from the things of the world. Or to put it this way, the soul of such a one is like a man who takes refuge in a stronghold so as to escape the attacks of an enemy.

The soul, in withdrawing the senses from exterior things, gains for itself clearer vision. So despicable do externals become that the eyes of the body unconsciously close, thereby excluding creatures. Thus, the gaze of the soul is more effectively focused on God. Wherefore those who follow this way nearly always pray with their eyes closed. And this is an excellent custom for many reasons. In the beginning, it is undoubtedly necessary to direct the gaze away from earthly objects. Later on, this effort will no longer be necessary. Quite to the contrary, when the soul is in the prayer of recollection, even more energy will have to be spent to keep the eyes open.

The soul now seems to realize that it has acquired strength and energy at the expense of the body, and that at last it is ready to rule that body which is now left alone and enfeebled. These effects are not very apparent in the beginning, because they are not very profound. Recollection, after all, may be developed to a greater or lesser degree. But let the soul, in accustoming itself to recollection, disregard its initial fatigue; for the body, anxious to reclaim its sway, will not concede that its plight comes from its unwillingness to admit defeat. If, with serious diligence, you continue in this manner for several days, you will clearly perceive what benefit you will derive from your efforts.

The soul will see that its faculties recollect themselves from the time that it applies itself to prayer, like bees who return to the hive to make honey. Nor will this cost it any effort whatsoever. Our Lord has arranged that during the time it did violence to itself, the soul gained ascendancy over the senses. Now, no sooner does the soul manifest its desire of recollection, than the senses straightway obey and become submissive. They wander again; but it is a great gain that they are now inclined to obey. Moreover, they now go forth only as subjects and captives, no longer capable of causing the soul vexation. If the will recalls them, the senses return with increasing swiftness. After they have thus often returned to recollection, our Lord will prepare the way for perfect contemplation.

Strive to comprehend well what I have just said. It may seem obscure, but when you put it into practice, you will understand. The souls who travel by this way seem to sail over the sea with speed. But since it is to our best interests to avoid all delay in attaining this prayerful practice of recollection, we shall now show briefly how we are to accustom ourselves to so excellent a means of progress.

Those persons who strive to become recollected are assuredly protected from many dangerous occasions. They are very quickly inflamed with the fire of divine love. Since they are near the fire, the least breath of the understanding is sufficient to cause the flames to engulf them entirely. Detached from exterior objects and being alone with God, they are admirably predisposed to become inflamed. I should wish you to have a very clear notion of this method of prayer. I have already stated that it is called the prayer of recollection.

The Heavenly Kingdom Within Us

Let us try to realize that we have within us a palace of ineffable splendor, built entirely of gold and precious gems; a dwelling worthy, in a word, of the Master to whom it belongs. Understand, moreover, that you in your own way really contribute to its grandeur; that there is no other palace whatsoever whose magnificence can be compared to that of a pure soul completely adorned with virtues; and that the more perfect these virtues, the more brilliantly do such gems shine. Represent to yourself the truth that within this palace dwells the great King who has, in his bounty, deigned to become your Father, and that he is seated on a throne of inestimable value, namely, your heart.

It may appear strange to you, at first, that I use such language, and employ such a figure of speech to help you understand the truth of which I speak. Nevertheless, it may well be very helpful, particularly to you. Women are inexperienced in lofty considerations of this kind, and thus need such concepts in order to understand perfectly that there is within the soul a treasure incomparably more precious than anything we can discern with the senses. Let us not imagine that the interior of our soul is empty. If only women were the only ones to hold this mistaken notion!

If we were careful to remember who is really the Guest of our soul, I think it would be impossible for us to become so attached to the things of the world. We should see how vile they are in comparison with the treasures we possess within us. But, alas, are we not like the animal which, at the sight of attractive prey, immediately rushes to satisfy its hunger? And nevertheless, what a difference there should be between the brute beast and us! Let us recall then, what a wonderful Father we have!

The Divine Indwelling

Perhaps some will laugh at me and say that this is an obvious truth. That is so; they are right. Nevertheless, for some time this truth remained obscure to me. I realized very well that I had a soul. But what I did not understand was the dignity of the soul, and the identity of its Guest, because the vanities of this life were like a film over my soul, blinding its vision. I did not realize then, as I do now, that a King of such Majesty dwelt within the small palace of my soul. Otherwise, it seems to me that I could never possibly have left him alone so often. At least, from time to time, I should have remained in his company, and should have watched with greater care that this palace be not tarnished.

But what could be more wonderful than to see him who could fill by his immensity thousands and thousands of worlds, enclose himself within a dwelling so small. So too, he had willed to be confined within the womb of his Most Holy Mother. In truth, he is the omnipotent Lord! And is he not free to act as he wills? Because he loves us, he accommodates himself to our capacity.

A soul, beginning in this way of prayer, would be dismayed to behold itself so small and insignificant, yet destined to receive within itself One who is infinite. But our Lord does not reveal himself to the soul immediately. He enlarges its capacity by degrees. He disposes it and prepares it for the gifts he intends to entrust to it. I said that he brings freedom of action with him, because he has infinite power to enlarge our hearts and to increase their capacity.

The Need for Total Detachment

What is important for us to learn is this: to give him as an outright gift this palace of our heart after we have emptied it of every created thing, so that he may dispose of it as his own possession. Since his Majesty is justified in wishing this self-emptying, let us not refuse him anything that he asks.

God does not force our will. He takes only what we give him. But he does not give himself entirely to us until we yield ourselves entirely to him. This is an absolute fact. Since this truth is exceedingly important, I cannot remind you of it often enough. Our Lord cannot act freely in the soul except when he finds it entirely detached from every creature and completely dedicated to himself. Without this, I cannot see how he could act, since he respects order so much. If we thus fill our palace with common rabble and with trifles, how can our Lord find a place there with his court? It would seem to be a gracious favor if he deigned to come even for one instant amid such confusion.

Charity of the Saints

And do you think he comes alone? Do you notice that his Son says of him, "Who art in heaven"? Would the courtiers of such a King leave him alone through carelessness? Assuredly not! They throng near him. They pray for all people and, because they are full of charity, they entreat him to lavish all graces upon us. Do not imagine that in heaven it is the same as it is on earth. Here below, princes and prelates cannot grant a favor to one person, whether for some special reasons, or simply from generous motives, without immediately arousing jealousy. And the unfortunate person thus honored is ill thought of, even though he has harmed no one. His favors have been dearly bought!

CHAPTER THREE

"WHO ART IN HEAVEN" *(concluded)*

The Fleeting Nature of Human Commendation

For the love of God, oh devoted souls in Christ, do not be anxious to receive from your superiors these favors of which we have just spoken. Each one of you should be intent upon doing your duty. If the superior does not manifest any sign of commendation, be assured that not only will our Lord be pleased, but that he will likewise reward you for it. Obviously, we did not come here to seek a reward in this life. Our thoughts, therefore, ought to be elevated to those things that endure forever. Do not place great value on terrestrial things that pass even more speedily than life itself.

The superior may be satisfied with the conduct of a certain sister today; tomorrow she may be even more satisfied with you, if she discerns greater virtue in you. But it is really of little consequence whether or not this happens. Do not indulge in such considerations. Sometimes thoughts of this kind begin with trifles, which may disturb you very much. Dismiss them without delay by recalling that your kingdom is not of this earth and that everything passes with surprising rapidity.

Abasement With Jesus

Nevertheless, this is not the highest motive, and does not indicate great perfection. It is preferable for you to remain always in disfavor and in abasement. Wish to remain thus for the love of our Lord, whom you find in abasement with you. Reflect upon yourselves and study your interior lives, as I have already advised. It is within you that you will find your Master who will never fail you. The more you are deprived of exterior consolations, the more he will lavish his joy upon you. He is full of compassion. He never abandons afflicted and lonely souls who place their entire trust in him. That is precisely why David said: "The Lord is near to the sad of heart" (cf. Ps 34:19). Either you believe this or you do not. But if you do, then why are you unduly anxious?

The Danger of Worldly Favors

Oh my Lord, nothing could cause us any anxiety if only we knew you well, who are truly magnanimous toward those who put their trust in you. Believe me, my friends, it is a great blessing to realize the truth of this. Only then does one see how truly deceptive all worldly favors are, when one realizes how they impede the soul, be it ever so little, from interior recollection. Who can make you understand this? Not I, assuredly. I admit that I have more reason to do so than any one else. Nevertheless, I am far from understanding it as I should.

Solitude With God in the Soul

I return to my subject. I should like to be able to explain to you how the heavenly cortege of the Saint of saints, who keeps you company, does not hinder the soul's solitude with its Beloved whenever the soul closes the door to all worldly things, and desires to enter into this paradise solely with its God. I say, whenever the soul desires this. Now realize this well, that there is no question here of the supernatural. This depends upon our will, and we can attain to it with the help of God. Without this help, however, nothing can be done; we cannot have even a single good thought.

The Realization of God's Presence in the Soul

I do not here speak of a silence of the faculties, but rather of a withdrawing of the powers to the interior of the soul. There are many ways of attaining this end. As some books advise, we must detach ourselves from everything in order to approach interiorly to God. Such is the teaching of those who discourse on mental prayer. But since I treat here only of the way in which to make vocal prayer well, it is not necessary for me to expound this point at length, as they do. I only wish to emphasize that we should realize with whom we speak and strive to remain in his presence without turning our backs on him. For that is what they do, who, while speaking to God, occupy themselves at the same time with a thousand frivolities.

It is indeed sad that anyone should fail to realize God's presence, but should imagine him to be afar off. He is truly at a great distance if we go to find him in heaven! But behold, oh Lord, here before us is your countenance! Should not he, then, who is so near us, be the object of our contemplation? It seems that people do not understand us if we do not look at one another while we are speaking. And still we close the eyes of our souls, oh my God, so as not to behold your glance on us! How can we know that you have listened to what we say?

Recollection of Exterior Senses

In order to train our spirits easily and surely to give heed to what is said and to whom we pray, what I want you to understand is only this, that we ought to recollect our exterior senses within us, and keep them thus engaged. It is by this means that we possess heaven within us, for the Master of heaven is found therein. And if we but once begin to realize by experience that it is not necessary to raise the voice to speak to him, inasmuch as his Majesty will have made his presence felt, we shall recite, with the greatest joy and ease, the Our Father and the other prayers which we wish.

In the midst of our occupations, we ought to withdraw into the interior of our souls, even though it be for just an instant, by reminding ourselves of him who keeps us company. This practice is extremely profitable. In brief, we ought to accustom ourselves to appreciate this truth, that it is not necessary to speak aloud to him, because his Majesty will make us feel his presence within us. In this way, we shall be able to recite our vocal prayers not only in peace, but without weariness as well.

After some time spent in generous efforts to keep ourselves in the company of our Lord, he will communicate with us by signs. Thus, whereas hitherto we felt that we had to recite the Our Father frequently to make ourselves understood, now he will indicate that he has heard us the first time, for he is most anxious to spare us the fatigue. If we recite the Our Father but once within the space of an hour, it is sufficient, provided on the one hand that we understand that we are with him, and know what we are asking of him; and on the other, that he be desirous of granting it, and that he derives great pleasure from our company. He does not like to have us rack our brains in addressing long discourses to him.

Prayerful Recitation of the Our Father

So, for the love of God, I implore you to accustom yourselves to recite the Our Father with recollection, and to draw as much profit from it as you can within a short space of time. As experience will soon teach you, this is a method that speedily helps the soul to avert the danger of losing its self-control, and to prevent its faculties from being dissipated. I beg you merely to give this a trial, even though it may at first cost you fatiguing effort; for everything is difficult until one becomes accustomed to it. But I can assure you that you will soon be consoled to realize that, without any fatiguing effort on your part, you will find within you the almighty Father to whom you pray. May it please his Majesty to teach this truth to those of you who are ignorant of it.

As for myself, I admit that I never knew what it was to pray in peaceful consolation until our Lord himself taught me this way. I have expounded this method at such great length here precisely because the habit of interior recollection has brought me the greatest benefits.

The Benefits of Interior Recollection

I conclude by saying that no one should be discouraged who wishes to arrive at this state of prayer, which I repeatedly insist is within our power. Let her accustom herself to it, as I said, and gradually she will gain self-mastery. Instead of dissipating her powers in aimless distractions, she will strive for mastery over self by forcing her faculties to recollection in the interior of her soul. If she speaks, let her remember that there is within her One with whom she can converse. If she listens, let her realize that she should hearken to him who speaks from the innermost recesses of her soul. In short, she will understand that if she but wish it, she need never separate herself from such holy companionship.

Frequent Recalling of Presence of God

Deeply will she lament whenever for any length of time she has deserted the Father whose assistance is so indispensable to her. Let her, then, recall his presence frequently during the day, or at least, from time to time. Let her accustom herself to the practice of this, and sooner or later, she will derive great profit from it. When she has finally obtained this grace from our Lord, she would not exchange it for all the treasures of the world.

Since all learning is to be gained at some cost, I entreat you, oh devoted souls of Christ, to consider as very well employed all your efforts in this regard. If you apply yourselves, I know that with the help of God, you will succeed after a year or perhaps even after six months. Realize how short a time this is to acquire a grace so well suited to become a solid foundation for those exalted things to which our Lord perhaps will deign to call you. Thus, by the very fact that you are close to him, will he find excellent dispositions in you. May it please his Majesty never to permit us to withdraw from his presence.

CHAPTER FOUR

"HALLOWED BE THY NAME"

Attention to Our Requests

Is there anyone, however thoughtless he may be, who when he desires a favor from an important person, does not study beforehand how to present his petition, in order to make a good impression and to avoid causing any displeasure? Should he not know what he desires, and what need he has of it, especially if he seeks an important favor, such as our good Jesus teaches us to request of him?

In my opinion, this is a point truly worthy of our attention. Could you not have comprised everything, oh my Lord, in a single phrase by saying, "Give us, oh Father, whatever we need"? That would have sufficed, it appears to me, since God knows everything so perfectly. Oh Eternal Wisdom, that one phrase would have been sufficient for you and for your Father! Thus it was that you prayed in the Garden of

Olives. You manifested to your Father your willingness and your fear, and then you submitted yourself to his will.

But, oh my Lord, you understand us too well to do this. You know that we are far from imitating your conformity to the will of the Father and that it is necessary for us to name each individual petition so that we might thus be inclined to consider whether our supplications were really good for us, and should they not be, to refrain from making them. We are so constituted that if we do not receive the gift we desire, our free will rejects the substitute our Lord wishes to give us, even though this might be better for us. Moreover, we never think we are rich unless we enjoy immediate possession of those things which we crave. Oh great God, how is it that our faith is so weak, and that we do not believe, for example, in the certainty of future punishments and rewards?

The Weakness of Our Faith

This weakness of faith is precisely the reason why you ought to know what you pray for in the Our Father, so that if the Eternal Father grants your petition, you will not reject his gift. Therefore, consider with the greatest care whether your petition would benefit you. If it would not, do not request it, but rather ask his Majesty to enlighten you. For we are blind, and our taste is not for the life-giving food, but rather for that which will cause our death. And what a terrifying and eternal death that is!

The good Jesus invites us to say those words by which we ask that the Kingdom of God should come to us, "Hallowed be thy name, thy kingdom come." Admire the infinite wisdom of our Master, and consider well just what we request when we pray for this kingdom. That is what I want to help you to do now.

His Majesty saw that, impeded by our natural weakness, we could not worthily hallow, praise, magnify, or glorify this blessed name of the Eternal Father unless he would deign to aid us by giving us his kingdom here on earth. Wherefore, the good Jesus placed these two petitions side by side, "Hallowed be thy name! Thy kingdom come!" By thus placing them together, he wishes to make us understand not only what we request, but also how important it is for us to be persevering in our entreaties without, however, neglecting to please him who is to grant the favor.

I should like to give you my opinion on this matter. If it is not suitable, you may make other considerations. Our Master permits you to do so, provided you submit everything to the teachings of the Church, as I always do. Nor will I give you this book to read until after it has been examined by competent persons. If it is not in conformity with the doctrine of the Church, that is due to my ignorance, not to any unworthy motive.

Peace in the Soul

This, then, is how I understand the ineffable joy which one receives together with many other blessings in the kingdom of heaven. The soul is no longer preoccupied in any way about the things of earth, for it finds peace and glory within itself. It rejoices at the happiness of all the other blessed, and the soul rests in perfect peace. Particularly is it gratified in seeing that all the elect, without any exception, praise our Lord and bless his holy name. Every soul in heaven loves him and is concerned with nothing else but loving him. Nor can the soul cease to love him, because it knows him as he is. Thus, too, should we love him here on earth, if we but knew him. Undoubtedly, we should not be able to do so with the same perfection, nor with the same constancy, as the blessed in heaven, but at least we should love him in an entirely different manner than we do now.

What I want to say is perhaps this: that we must be angels in order to make this petition and to pray well vocally. Assuredly, this is what our divine Master wishes, since he directs us to make a prayer so sublime. And since he would not oblige us to request impossibilities, we can be certain that a soul living in this exile can obtain this grace from God. True, it will never succeed in loving God with the perfection of those souls already liberated from the prison of the body, for we are still voyaging by sea and continuing on a journey. Nevertheless, there are moments when our Lord, seeing the soul wearied on its journey route, puts first the powers of the soul at rest, and then the soul itself in a state of peace. Next, by certain signs, he clearly shows to the soul why it thus enjoys a foretaste of the favor reserved for those who already inhabit the heavenly kingdom. When he grants this grace, which we all request, he simultaneously gives such pledges of love that the soul becomes confident that it will enjoy for all eternity what it is permitted to taste but rarely here on earth.

If you would not accuse me of discoursing on contemplation, this petition of the Our Father would afford me an excellent occasion to speak to you a little about the first stage of pure contemplation, which is called by those favored with it, the prayer of quiet. But as I have already stated, I intend here to speak only of vocal prayer, and well might it seem to the inexperienced that these forms of prayer are not compatible.

Nevertheless, I know personally that they are. Forgive me then, if I speak of this subject.

Prayer of Pure Contemplation

I know many persons who pray vocally, as I have explained, whom God raises, unknown to themselves, to a high degree of contemplation. This is why I am so insistent that you recite your vocal prayers well. I know one such person in particular who could pray only vocally; but in being faithful to vocal prayer, she enjoyed all the rest as well. If she did not pray vocally, she became so distracted that it was an ordeal for her. And would to God that we made our mental prayer as perfectly as she did her vocal prayer! She would spend several hours in reciting some Our Fathers and a few other prayers, at the same time meditating on the mysteries of the passion of our Lord.

One day she came to me exceedingly disconsolate because she knew not, as she said, how to make mental prayer, and being unable to raise herself to contemplation, she did nothing else but recite vocal prayers. I questioned her as to her manner of reciting these prayers, and I perceived that, being faithful to the recitation of the Our Father, she had arrived at the prayer of pure contemplation. Our Lord raised her even to the prayer of union. It was evident from her conduct that she had received the highest favors in prayer, for she led a very saintly life. I could not help but praise our Lord, and always will. I envy her such vocal prayer. Now if this is so, and I assure you that it is, then you who are mistrustful of contemplatives should not believe that you yourselves will not become such if you recite your prayers properly and with a pure conscience.

Chapter Five

"THY KINGDOM COME"

The Prayer of Quiet

I shall now explain the prayer of quiet, as I have heard it expounded or as our Lord has deigned to make me understand it, in order, doubtlessly, that I in turn may explain it to you. In my opinion, it is precisely in this prayer, as I have previously stated, that our Lord manifests to us that he hears our petition. He begins to give us his kingdom here on earth, so that we can truly praise him, hallow his name, and strive finally to make all creatures praise and glorify his name. This prayer is a supernatural favor and quite beyond all our combined efforts, no matter how great they may be.

The soul now enters into perfect peace, or to speak more exactly, our Lord by his presence bestows peace upon it, as he did to the holy man, Simeon. All its faculties are in repose. In a way that far exceeds the powers of its exterior faculties, it realizes that it is very close to its God, and that if it were to draw but a little nearer, it would become one with him through union. Still, it sees him neither with the eyes of the body nor with those of the soul. The holy Simeon, when he gazed on the glorious infant Jesus, saw nothing more than a poor child. Had he judged him only from the swaddling clothes and from his few attendants, he would have taken him for some poor little pilgrim rather than for the Son of the heavenly Father. But the divine Infant made himself known to Simeon.

In this same manner, God reveals himself to the soul on earth, though not with the same clarity, for the soul does not yet know how it recognizes God. It merely sees that it is in the kingdom, or at least near the King who will bestow the kingdom. It is overwhelmed with such a spirit of reverence that it dares not ask anything of him. It is as though the interior and exterior faculties were suspended.

And that you may better understand me, by the exterior person I mean the body, which does not wish to stir. It is like the traveler who takes some rest near the journey's end and derives from this rest the strength and courage to continue on. While the body experiences great delight, the soul experiences a sublime beatitude. Indeed, the soul is so happy at merely seeing itself near the heavenly Fountain that, even before it has quenched its thirst, it is ravished with joy. It imagines that there is nothing more to desire. Its faculties are in such a state of quiet that they are reluctant to stir; so much so, in fact, that everything seems to prevent it from even making an act of love. Nevertheless, the faculties are not so completely suspended that they do not think of him in whose presence they are.

Two of the faculties remain free. The will alone is captive and the only pain that it can now experience is the thought that it will regain its former freedom. The understanding wishes to comprehend but one object, and the memory is concerned about one thing only. Both see that one thing alone is necessary, and that anything else may only disturb them.

Those who are in this state do not want the body to stir, for fear of losing this peace. Hence it is that they do not dare to make the least movement. It is difficult for them to speak. The recitation of only one Our Father would require an hour. But since they are so near to God, signs are sufficient for this mutual communication. There in the palace near the King, they realize that even here on earth he begins to bestow upon them his kingdom. In a word, they seem no longer to belong to this world.

They wish neither to see nor to listen to the world, but only to see and listen to their God. Nothing troubles them, and in my opinion, nothing ought ever trouble them again. In short, during the time of this joy and intimate happiness, their faculties are so enraptured and absorbed that they cannot call to mind anything more to be desired. Quite willingly would they repeat with St. Peter: "Lord, let us set up here three tabernacles" (cf. Mt 17:4).

Sometimes during this prayer of quiet, God grants another favor that is very difficult to understand; at least it is so when one is not favored with it frequently. But anyone who has had such an experience will understand my explanation at once and be happy to derive from it an exact knowledge of the nature of this favor. Moreover, I believe that God frequently bestows this favor simultaneously with the one we have just considered.

When the quietude is profound and prolonged, the will, according to my understanding of it, cannot remain long in this state of repose, unless it is held by some object. Now it so happens that we do continue in this state for a day or so without our comprehending how it takes place. I speak of those who enjoy this great favor. They clearly realize that they are not entirely absorbed in their exterior occupations. And that is because the most important thing of all, their will, is not in their work. In my opinion, the will unites itself wholly to God, and leaves the other faculties free to busy themselves in the service of his glory. For this, they possess exceptional aptitude, whereas in matters of worldly concern, they are without ability and are sometimes even stupid.

This surely is a great grace. Here both the active and the contemplative life function harmoniously together. Everything in us unites to further the glory of God. The will, rapt in contemplation, is busy at its tasks without knowing how it works, while the other faculties perform the duties of Martha. Thus Martha and Mary proceed together.

I know a person to whom God often granted this grace. Since she did not understand it, she asked a great contemplative about it. He informed her that such a thing was quite possible and that it likewise happened to him. Since the will enjoys such entire satisfaction in this prayer of quiet, I think that during most of the time it must be united to him who alone is able to satisfy it.

It would be helpful here, it seems to me, to make a few remarks to those among you whom our Lord, solely out of his beneficence, raises to this state. And I know there are several of you thus favored.

The Supernatural Nature of This Favor

At the outset, note that some persons, when they find themselves favored with this joy, the source of which they are unable to discern though they realize that at least it exceeds their own powers, are tempted nevertheless to imagine that they can prolong it. And thus they do not wish even to breathe. What folly! This favor is no more under our control than the coming of day or night. It is entirely supernatural and beyond all our efforts. The best means of prolonging it is to realize clearly that we can neither add to it nor subtract from it, that we are altogether unworthy of it, and that we ought to accept it with gratitude, not by speaking much, but, like the publican, by raising our eyes to heaven.

It is good at such a time to seek greater solitude, so as to give our Lord more freedom to act in our soul, just as he would act in his own domain. At most, it will be necessary to utter an occasional aspiration. This will act like the gentle breath that rekindles a dying ember, but which would have extinguished a burning light. I say a gentle breath lest, in formulating many words with our mind, we distract the will.

Pay special attention, my friends, to this other counsel I am now about to give you. You will often discover that during this time, you are unable to use either the understanding or the memory. Sometimes it happens that the understanding is very much disturbed while the soul is in profound quietude. It seems that what is happening does not take place in its own abode; it imagines itself to be a dissatisfied guest in a strange house. And so in its restiveness it goes in search of other lodgings. Perhaps the circumstance belongs only to my case, and other persons may not have the same trouble. If so, I speak only of myself. Sometimes I even want to die, because of my powerlessness to control the instability of my understanding.

At other times, it seems to settle down at home in company with the will. When the three faculties are in harmonious agreement, the soul is in a state of bliss. Then conditions resemble the life of a happy married couple who love one another and agree perfectly in their tastes. But should the husband be disagreeable, you know what unhappiness he can cause his wife.

When the will is in this quietude, it should not pay any more attention to the understanding than it would to an idiot. For if the will wishes to draw this faculty to itself, it will necessarily be distracted and somewhat disquieted, and from all its efforts, it will gain nothing else but fatigue. On the contrary, it will lose what our Lord bestows without requiring of it any effort.

Give heed to this comparison, which appears to me quite exact, and which our Lord suggested to me one day while I was in this prayer. During the prayer of quiet, the soul is like an infant at its mother's breast who receives its nourishment without any effort whatsoever on its part. This is the image of what happens here. Without any effort whatsoever on the part of the understanding, the will is preoccupied in loving. Our Lord desires that the will, without any explicit effort, should understand that it is in his presence, and that its sole preoccupation is to drink with joy the milk that his Majesty places in its mouth. He wishes it to know that he himself bestows this grace and to rejoice in its happiness, but not to strive to fathom the manner of this enjoyment, nor the nature of this bliss. It should forget entirely about itself; he who remains close will not fail to provide everything that is necessary. But if the will undertakes to draw the understanding to itself by force and to make it share its own happiness, it will meet with failure. Moreover, during this struggle, it will necessarily let some of this milk of exhilarating consolation fall from its lips, and so lose this divine nourishment.

The difference between this prayer of quiet and that wherein the soul is entirely united to God is that in the latter, there is no need to swallow the nourishment. The soul finds its food within itself, without knowing how our Lord placed it there. In the prayer of quiet, on the contrary, our Lord seems to leave a little work for the soul to do. This work, however, is done with such peace that the soul is hardly conscious of any exertion. What annoys it at this time is the understanding. But when there is union of the three faculties, this does not happen, for he who created them suspends their natural activity. He lavishes such joy upon them that he takes them out of themselves without their perceiving or discerning how this is done.

When the soul is raised to the prayer of quiet, it experiences a peaceful and profound contentment in the will. It would not know how to describe accurately the nature of this favor, it is true. But it can at least perceive that it is decidedly different from all terrestrial joys, and that all the pleasures of the world could not cause this transport of joy that is in the interior of the will. For earthly joys, it seems to me, affect only the exterior of the surface of the will.

Once the soul has been raised to this high degree of prayer, which I repeat is manifestly supernatural, it should not be disturbed if the understanding should be taken up with the most extravagant musings. Let the soul laugh at it, treat it as an idiot, and remain tranquil, whilst the reveries come and go. Here the will is sovereign, in command, and can recall the imagination without pursuing it. If the will tries forcibly to bring it back, it will lose the mastery over it, which it derives from its heavenly food. Neither the will nor the understanding would profit thereby, but both would be the losers.

There is a saying, "Whoever reaches for too much, grasps nothing," which seems to me to apply to the subject we are considering. Your own experience will enable you to understand this. But if you have had none, I can well understand that my words appear obscure and my advice futile. But I repeat that even with a little experience, you will be able to understand my counsel and profit by it. Then you will thank our Lord for having granted me the grace to expound the matter here.

In conclusion, I would say that the soul elevated to this degree of prayer may well believe that the Eternal Father has already granted its request, and bestowed upon it his kingdom here on earth. Oh blessed petition, wherein, without knowing it, we beg so great a good! Oh blessed form of prayer! It is precisely because of this that I desire that we should know how to recite this prayer of the Our Father and all our other vocal prayers.

When God bestows such a favor upon a soul, it should not be concerned about worldly matters. When the Master of the world visits the soul, he banishes all creatures from it. I do not say that all those who enjoy this grace are thereby entirely detached from everything. I want them at least to realize that they still need to humble themselves and to strive to live in absolute detachment. Otherwise, they will make no progress.

The Necessity of Faithfulness to Grace

When a soul receives such pledges of love, it is a sign that God calls it to great things. And unless it be unfaithful to grace, it will make admirable progress. But if God sees that the soul returns to worldly things after he has established his kingdom within it, not only will he cease to reveal the mysteries of his kingdom, but in the future, he will grant this grace only at rare intervals and for very brief spaces of time.

It is possible that I am mistaken on this point; nevertheless, I see and know that this is what happens. Moreover, I am convinced that this is the reason why many souls do not rise higher in the spiritual life. They do not conform their conduct to so great a grace, and they do not dispose themselves to receive new favors from our Lord's hands. As they withdraw their will, which he considered his own, and center it on base things, God in turn will seek other souls who will love him truly, so that he may bestow upon them even more sublime favors. Still he does not entirely deprive these others of the favors previously bestowed, provided they live with a pure conscience.

The Great Danger of Hurried Vocal Prayers

There are, however, some persons, and I was among this number, whom our Lord fills with sentiments of devotion, to whom he suggests holy inspirations, to whom he may give light to perceive the nothingness of all earthly things, upon whom, finally, he even bestows his kingdom in this prayer of quiet, and yet who still remain deaf to his voice. And would you like to know the reason for this? It is because they are so concerned about reciting a specified number of vocal prayers that they rush through these prayers in order to be able to acquit themselves of the number they have resolved upon for each day. And thus I repeat, that though our Lord, by means of this prayer of quiet and this interior peace, puts into their hands his kingdom, nevertheless they do not receive it. They are mistakenly persuaded that it is better to recite vocal prayers. Thus they spurn this favor.

Do not act this way. Be aware of this grace when our Lord bestows this inestimable favor upon you. Otherwise, you will lose a precious treasure. Realize that you accomplish much more by pronouncing one single word of the Our Father from time to time than by frequently and distractedly repeating the whole prayer in haste. He to whom you pray is very close to you. He will not fail to hear you. Believe me, you will thus truly hallow and sanctify his name. You will then glorify our Lord as a member of his household should glorify him. You will praise him with greater love and zeal. And finally, you will feel that you can never cease working for his glory. This is my advice to you. Consider it well, for it is very important.

CHAPTER SIX

"THY WILL BE DONE ON EARTH, AS IT IS IN HEAVEN"

Fulfillment of the Divine Will

Our good Master has interceded for us and has taught us to ask favors of such value that they really comprise all that we can desire in this world. He has even conferred upon us the inestimable favor of making us his brothers and sisters. Let us now see what he wishes us to give to his Father in return, what he offers him on our behalf, and what he requests of us. It is only right that we should do something in return for such great graces.

Oh great Jesus, that which you receive from us is of little value in comparison with that which you request for us. And this little, is it not in itself absolute nothingness in comparison with what we owe such a Sovereign as you are? Nevertheless, my Lord, it is certain that you not leave us devoid of everything, for we give all we can when we sincerely offer all that is expressed in the words, "Thy will be done on earth, as it is in heaven."

Oh good Master, you have done well in presenting to your Father this petition so that we may have the means of fulfilling what you give in our name. Otherwise, oh Lord, I am certain it would be impossible for us to do so. But since your Father, in answer to your request, grants us his kingdom here below, I know that we shall not disappoint you. We shall fulfill whatever you promise for us. From the moment that my soul, worldly though it be, is transformed into a heaven, your will can be fulfilled in me. Otherwise, of what could clay as base and fruitless as mine be capable? I truly wonder, oh Lord, for it is a great gift you offer in our name.

Absurd Fear of Trials

When I think of this, I am amused at those persons who dare not beg trials from God, for fear of being heard immediately. I do not speak of those who refrain from doing so in the spirit of humility because they imagine they could not stand the trials. Nevertheless, I am convinced that he who grants us sufficient love to enable us to implore so arduous a means to prove our devotedness, will at the same time give us sufficient love to enable us to suffer with courage.

I should like to learn from those who do not request trials for fear of being heard immediately, what precisely they wish to express when they beg our Lord to fulfill his will in them. Do they say these words just because everyone does, but without the intention of conforming their lives to his will in practice? That surely would not be right.

Do you see, therefore, how our good Jesus becomes our ambassador in this way? Did he not wish to be the Mediator between us and his Father? And certainly this has cost him dearly! It would not be right, then, to fail to realize what he offers in our name. If we do not wish to realize this, let us not make the petition.

Inevitable Fulfillment of the Divine Will

Consider attentively, too, oh devoted friends of Christ, this other reason. Whether we wish it or not, God's will must of necessity be fulfilled in heaven and on earth. Believe me, take my advice, and make a virtue of necessity.

Oh my Lord, what an ineffable grace it is for me that you have not left the accomplishment of your divine will to the mercy of such a weak will as mine!

May you be forever blessed! May all creatures praise you! May your name be glorified eternally! Oh my Lord, what a disaster it would be if the accomplishment of your will depended on me! But now I freely offer you my will, even though it may not be devoid of self-interest. From long experience, I know what profit I derive from resigning my will freely to yours. What advantages I gain from this! And on the other hand, when we present this petition of the Our Father, what a loss it would be if we were to fail to accomplish what we offer to our Lord.

The Sublime Grandeur of Offering of the Will

Before speaking of the advantages you gain by this, I should like to show you the sublime grandeur of this offering in itself. From now on, at least, you cannot say that you did not understand it and that you were in error about it. Do not imitate certain nuns who make promises but never fulfill them. Because they do nothing about them, they allege that when they made these promises, they did not understand the meaning of their obligations. This I readily believe. It is indeed easy to talk but difficult to act. If anyone believes that words and deeds were the same, that person most certainly lacks understanding. Therefore, put to a long test those who would make their profession in this convent in order to convince them that they must never be satisfied with vain promises, but they must prove their earnestness by their deeds. In this matter of reciting the Our Father, my wish is that you may well understand with whom you are dealing. Realize therefore what it is that the good Jesus offers to his Father for you, and what it is that you give him when you request him to fulfill his will in you.

It appears very easy to say that one yields one's will to the authority of another. But when the real test comes, one realizes that there is nothing in the world quite so difficult as to submit one's will as one ought. Superiors do not always command us with inflexibility, because they know our weakness. Sometimes, however, they treat the weak and strong alike. But our Lord does not act in this way. He knows exactly how much each creature can bear. When, therefore, he finds a valiant soul, he does not hesitate to accomplish in it his will.

Suffering, the Real Meaning of Divine Will

I should like to explain to you what the will of God really is. Have no fear that our Lord wishes to bestow upon you riches, pleasures, honors, or any other worldly goods. He loves you too much and he values your gifts too highly for that. That is why he wishes to provide for you adequately and to give you his kingdom even in this life.

Would you like to know how he treats those who sincerely request him to fulfill his will in them? Ask his glorious Son who addressed this very petition to him in the Garden of Olives. With the firm resolve to carry it out, he courageously petitioned the Father to accomplish in him his holy will. And see how his Father did so, when he delivered him up to all forms of trials, sufferings, insults, and persecutions, even to the extent of permitting him to die on the Cross.

Love, the Measure of the Cross

In seeing what the Father bestowed upon him whom he loved above all others, you realize what his will means. These are the gifts he bestows upon us in this world. He proportions them according to his love for us. To those whom he loves more, he grants more, and less to those whom he loves less. But at the same time, he regulates their distribution according to the courage and love he finds in each one of us. He sees that when one loves him much, one can suffer much for him, but when one loves him little, one can endure but little for him. Personally, I am convinced that love is the real measure of the cross that we can bear, be this cross great or small. That is why if you possess this love, you will take care that, in addressing so great a Lord, your words be not empty compliments. Nor will you omit anything that will enable you to accept the crosses that his Majesty deigns to send you.

Precious Jewel

If you do not give him your will in this manner, you are like a person who shows a friend a precious jewel, not only offering it to him, but even entreating him to accept it. And yet, when the friend stretches out his hand to take the jewel, the would-be donor draws it back. Surely these are not the kind of hollow mockeries to practice on him who has borne so much for us!

Were there no other reason than this, it would not be fair to treat him heedlessly so often, for it is very frequently that we address this petition to him in the Our Father. Let us give him then, once and for all, this precious jewel that we have so long pretended to proffer him. For if our Lord does not give himself to us first, he acts thus in order that we may anticipate him with the gift of our will.

Oh great God, how perfectly Jesus, our only Good, seems to know us! It is not at the beginning of the Our Father that he tells us to give our will to God. He waits until we have been generously rewarded for this service. And this service is truly trivial when one realizes the immense advantages our Lord wants us to find herein. For even in this life, he begins to reward us, as I shall now undertake to explain.

The Difference Between Words and Deeds

Persons who live in the world indeed accomplish much if they have a firm determination to keep their promise. But you, oh devoted friends of Christ, cannot be content merely to promise; you must act. From you are demanded not merely words, but deeds. And in very truth, it is precisely this that is expected of every religious soul. Sometimes, however, it happens that after promising our Lord the precious jewel, and even after placing it in his hands, we take it back again. At first we show much generosity, but afterward we become so ungenerous that perhaps it would have been better had we been less hasty in our offering.

The sole aim of all the advice I have given you in this book has been to lead you to abandon yourselves entirely to the Creator, to submit your will to him, and to detach yourselves from creatures. Before now you have understood its tremendous importance, so I shall not treat it at length here.

The Entire Gift of Self

I wish merely to tell you why our good Master places here the words of the petition, "Thy will be done." Well he knows that nothing is more profitable for us than the glory we give to the Eternal Father by giving ourselves entirely to him. In this way, we prepare ourselves to arrive speedily at the destination of our journey and to drink the living water at the Fountain of which we spoke. But if we do not surrender our will completely to our Lord, so that he can dispose of it entirely as he sees fit, he will never permit us to drink from this Sacred Fountain.

It is in this that the perfect contemplation of which you asked me to speak consists. And here, as I have already said, we can offer nothing on our part, neither effort, nor ingenuity, nor anything whatsoever. For all that we should like to do would trouble our soul and would hinder our saying, "Thy will be done."

Courageous Acceptance of Crosses

Grant, oh Lord, that your will may be done in me! That your will may be fulfilled in every way and in every manner that pleases you, oh my Lord! If you will it to be in the midst of trials, give me, then, the strength to bear them, and then let come what may. If you will that there be persecutions, infirmities, humiliations, and want, behold I stand before you, oh my Father. I will not refuse them. It would not be right to flee from them.

Since your Son, speaking in the name of all, has offered you my will along with the others, I could not fail on my part to give you what he promised in my name. But deign to give me that kingdom of yours that he requested for me, so I may be equal to such an undertaking. Then, oh my God, dispose of me as of an object that is entirely yours, according to your good pleasure.

What power, oh devoted friends of Christ, this gift contains! If it is offered with fitting generosity, it cannot fail to induce the Omnipotent God to become one with our lowliness in order to transform us into himself, to unite the Creator with the creature. See how well repaid you will be. Realize how munificent your Master is. He knows well how one can gain his Father's affection. He teaches us the means by which to glorify him.

The more our Lord sees that the gift of ourselves consists not in hollow complimentary phrases, but in deeds, the closer does he draw to us, elevating our soul above itself and above the things of this world, so as to prepare it to receive even greater favors. He values this gift so highly that he never ceases to reward us for it, even in this life.

The State of Rapture

He showers so many favors upon the soul that it does not know what to request from him. In truth, his Majesty never tires of bestowing favors. Not content with uniting this soul to himself, the divine Master begins to fill it with special graces and to reveal to it his secrets. He is pleased at the soul's appreciation of his treasures, and its anticipation of what still remains for it. Gradually, he suspends the activity of the exterior senses so that nothing will hold it back. This state is called rapture.

God begins to manifest such signs of intimate friendship to the soul that he gives it back not only its will, but bestows his own will as well. When he acts toward it in this fashion, he takes delight in seeing the two wills alternate, as it were, in the privilege of mastery. He accedes to all the wishes of the soul, just as it, in turn, fulfills his commands. His manner of acting, however, is far superior because on the one hand being omnipotent, he can do everything he wills, and on the other, he never ceases to will. The poor soul would desire to will in this way, but it cannot accomplish what it wills. In fact, it can do nothing without an outright gift from God. Its greatest asset consists precisely in this, that the more perfectly it serves God, the more indebted it becomes to him.

Oftentimes, the soul is tormented when it sees itself subject to the many inconveniences, obstacles, and bonds it discovers in the prison of the body, for it would gladly acquit at least a part of its debts. It is really absurd to be thus afflicted. Even if the soul did everything it could, it would still be utterly powerless to give anything that it had not previously received. It is really capable of only one thing, that is, to acknowledge humbly its poverty, to accomplish perfectly what depends on it, and to make the gift of its will. All else retards and actually harms the soul instead of bringing benefits to the soul raised to this state by our Lord.

The Great Importance of Humility

Humility alone can be helpful here. The humility of which I speak is not acquired by means of the understanding, but is derived from the clear evidence of the truth. It makes the soul understand in one moment what it could not have gained by many years of reflection, namely, the abyss of its nothingness and the incomparable Majesty of God.

I wish to give you additional counsel. Do not think that you can arrive at this state by your own efforts and undertakings. You will never attain it by your own powers. You could perhaps enjoy devotion for a while, but your ardor would not continue for long. Speak, then, with simplicity and humility, for humility gains everything. "Thy will be done."

CHAPTER SEVEN

"GIVE US THIS DAY OUR DAILY BREAD"

Fulfillment of the Will of God

As I have stated, our good Jesus understood the great difficulty we should experience in accomplishing what he promised his Father on our behalf. He likewise knew our weakness and how, because of our tendency to pretend not to understand the will of God, he would be obliged, in his goodness, to aid us in our need. Failure on our part to fulfill what he promised in our name would in no way redound to our credit, because all favors have been given us in view of this promise. However, he realized how difficult a task it is for us.

Tell a person living in the midst of luxuries and riches, for instance, that the will of God demands that he moderate the excesses of his table in order to give bread, at least, to those who are dying of hunger, and he will find a thousand pretexts for not heeding you or for interpreting the injunction according to his preferences. Tell the detractor that the will of God enjoins that we love our neighbor as ourselves, and he will pay no heed to your counsel or to any other convincing argument.

Conscientious Observance of Religious Rule

Tell a self-willed and self-indulgent religious that he must give good example; that he cannot limit himself to mere lip service in pronouncing the prayer, "Thy will be done"; that he has promised and even vowed to fulfill this divine will; that it is the will of God that he should be faithful to his vows; that he sins seriously against his vows if he gives scandal, even though he might not violate them completely; that he has made the vow of poverty, and that he is bound to observe it loyally, because it is the will of God. Explain all this, and yet even today you will find some whom you cannot possibly lead back to better dispositions. What would have happened then, had our Lord not reduced the greater part of the difficulty by the remedy he granted us? Indeed there would have been very few capable of fulfilling the petition he addressed to his Father in our name when he said, "Thy will be done."

The Profound Significance of the Words of Jesus

The good Jesus, seeing how essential his help was to us, sought an admirable means to manifest his ineffable love for us. Hence, in his own name, and in that of his brethren, he prayed, "Give us this day our daily Bread." For the love of God, oh devoted friends of Christ, let us realize the deep significance of these words of our good Master. Let us not hurry lightly over this petition, for it deals with the very life of our soul. Do not attach great importance to what you have given our Lord, because there is really no comparison possible between your gift and the rich reward you are going to receive from him.

This is a thought that comes to me at the moment, but which I submit to the better judgment of others: the good Jesus knew what he promised in our name and how important it would be for us to realize this. Furthermore, he perfectly understood the difficulty this promise would entail because of our weakness, our attraction to worldly objects, our lack of love, and our want of courage. Consequently, he would have to arouse our love by keeping his own Love before our eyes, not only on one day, but every day. That is why he resolved to remain in our midst.

The Presence of Jesus in Our Midst

Considering, however, the gravity and importance of the matter, he wished this favor to come from the hand of his Eternal Father. Obviously, he is One with his almighty Father. He knew that his Father would ratify and heartily approve in heaven whatever he, the Son, did on earth since the divine will is one. Nevertheless, the humility of the good Jesus was so profound that he wished, so to speak, to ask the permission of his Father, though he well realized the infinite love and complaisance of his Father toward him. He fully understood that the present petition was more important than the preceding one, because he foresaw the death to which he would be condemned and the insults and outrages he would have to suffer.

But, dear Lord, who is the Father who would permit the wondrous Son he has given us to remain among us to suffer new outrages every day, when he has already seen him so cruelly treated? Assuredly, no other Father except your own would have permitted this. Well did you know to whom it was you addressed this petition, oh my God, what infinite love in the Son, and what boundless love in the Father!

Nevertheless, I am amazed at the good Jesus. Once he had uttered the words, "Thy will be done," he was obliged to fulfill them in a manner worthy of God. Surely, he is not like us. He fully realized that he accomplished the will of his Father in loving us as he loves himself. And thus he endeavored to fulfill this will in the most perfect manner, no matter what the sacrifice entailed might cost him.

Profanations Against Jesus in the Blessed Sacrament

Eternal Father, how did you ever permit this? How do you consent to deliver your Son each day into such wicked hands as ours? You delivered him up once, upon his own request, and you witnessed the frightful indignities heaped upon him. How can your tender love bear to see him exposed to such outrages each and every day? Alas, what terrible profanations are being committed against him this very day in the Blessed Sacrament! In how many hostile hands must his Father behold him! And how innumerable are the profanations of the unfortunate heretics!

Oh Eternal Sovereign, how can you consent to such a petition? How can you grant it? Do not permit yourself to be swayed by his love. He is so eager to accomplish your will and to labor for our salvation, that he would be ready to be torn to pieces every day. You, oh Father, have the responsibility to guard the interests of your Son, because nothing can check the ardor of his love. Why is it that all the blessings that come to us should be charged to his account? Why does he suffer in silence all the outrages heaped upon him? Why does he never speak for himself or open his lips except to plead our cause? Is there no one to plead for this loving Lamb?

Boundless Love of Jesus for Us

I cannot help but note with admiration that only in this petition does he repeat the same words. In the first part, he prays for our daily bread, and then adds, "Give it to us today, oh Lord."

It is as though he said to his Father that we should not be deprived of him, who became our good by delivering himself to death once for us, but that he should be given to us until the end of time.

This consideration, oh devoted friends of Christ, should touch your hearts with gratitude and fill them with love for your divine Guest. Where is there a slave who glories in his servitude? And still the good Jesus considers it an honor to be our slave.

Oh Eternal Father, how exceedingly meritorious must this humility be! What treasure is precious enough to purchase your Son for us? We know that thirty pieces of silver sufficed to sell him. But no sum is sufficient to buy him back.

Because he possesses our nature, he unites himself with us here. But since he is Master of his own will, he reminds his Father that he is entitled to give himself to us. That is why he says, "Our bread." He thus makes no distinction between himself and us. It is we who do so, when we refuse to give his Majesty our will every day.

Chapter Eight

"GIVE US THIS DAY OUR DAILY BREAD" (continued)

The Sublime Meaning of This Petition

It seems that when our Lord asks for daily bread, he means to ask it for all eternity. But then this thought comes to me. Why does our Lord, after saying "Every day," add "Give us this day our daily bread"? In my opinion, "Our daily bread" means that if we take care to profit by his company, we shall have this bread not only on earth, but also in heaven. For he abides with us solely to aid, encourage, and sustain us so that the will of his Father may be accomplished in us.

But when he says "this day," it seems to me to mean a single day; the day, that is, of this world's duration. In truth, the world lasts but a day, especially for those poor unfortunate ones who, because they are condemned to hell, will not enjoy this bread in the next life. If they permit themselves to be overcome, it is not the fault of our Savior, who, to the very end of life's combat, never ceases to encourage them. They will have no reason then for making excuses for themselves, neither can they accuse the Eternal Father of having deprived them of this bread when they most needed it.

The Son says to his Eternal Father, "Since the world lasts but one day, permit me to pass it in servitude." And so God the Father, of his own will, has given him to us and has sent him into this world. The Son, in turn, of his own will, does not wish to abandon us but to abide with us for the greater glory of his friends and to the discomfiture of his enemies.

The Blessed Bread of Heaven

Notice that our Lord makes this new petition only for "this day." The Eternal Father has given us this sacred bread. And I repeat that he gives us for all time this blessed bread of the sacred humanity, which is genuine manna for us, always corresponding to our tastes and needs. We shall never die of hunger, except through our own fault. Our soul can find in the Most Blessed Sacrament all the joys and consolations it desires. There are no privations, trials, or persecutions that are not easy to bear once we begin to contemplate those of our Savior, to love them, and to share them.

I cannot bring myself to believe that our Lord referred to that other bread, which sustains and repairs the bodily forces. Nor should I wish you to think of it thus. The bread of which he speaks in this passage is that which is tasted in the highest form of contemplation. Once the soul has reached this state, it is no more occupied about the world than if it were not living on this earth. For far greater reason, then, does it forget entirely about bodily food.

Would it be necessary for our Lord to emphasize material nourishment? For his honor and our own, let us not adhere to this interpretation. He teaches us to direct our wills to heavenly things and to beg that we be permitted, in this exile, to begin to taste of these joys. Should he then be obliged to persuade us to request something so commonplace as food, as though he did not know our human weakness? On the contrary, he knew only too well that if once we began to be concerned about our bodily needs, we should forget those of the soul.

In union with our Lord, oh devoted friends of Christ, ask the Eternal Father to leave your divine Guest with you this day, and never in this world to separate you from him. That he remains hidden beneath the appearance of bread and wine is already sufficient to moderate so great a joy. For one who loves nothing else in this world, and who finds no consolation elsewhere, this is even a great hardship. Beg him to fail you not, and to prepare you to receive him worthily.

Complete Abandonment to the Divine Will

If you have completely abandoned yourselves to the will of God, do not give thought during your prayers to any other kind of bread. You have more important matters to treat during those moments. There are appropriate times when the person to whom this duty is confided will see to it that you have sufficient food to eat, or rather, will share with you what is available. Fear not! Our Lord will not fail you, unless you first fail him in that total surrender of yourself to the divine will, which you have made. And I unhesitatingly assure you that if I were to fail on this point through my own fault, I would never beg anything more from him, neither bread nor any other food. I would rather that he let me die of hunger. Why should I desire to prolong my life if each additional day meant nothing else but the ratification of the sentence to eternal death?

There are stated times designated for work and the gaining of livelihood, but never be preoccupied about the means of your subsistence. Let the body work, for it is fitting that you should work for your support. But let the soul be at peace during your work. As I have previously told you at length, leave the care of temporalities to your Maker. He will never abandon you.

The Relationship of Master and Servant

You are like a servant who aims to please his master in everything. In return, the master is bound to furnish food for the servant unless the former becomes so poor that he is unable to support either himself or his servant. But our case is different, for our Master is rich and powerful. Hence, it is not fitting that we, his servants, should request food from him. We know very well that our Master takes care of us and will always do so. With truth he can say to us, "Be intent upon serving and pleasing me. For if your solicitude extends to matters that do not concern you, you will do nothing in a satisfactory manner."

Longing for Heavenly Food

Oh devoted friends of Christ, let those who wish, ask for material bread. As for us, let us beg the Eternal Father that we may merit to receive our heavenly food with such dispositions that even though we have not the happiness to contemplate our hidden God with our bodily eyes, we may at least see him unveiled to the eyes of our soul. This heavenly bread is an entirely superior kind of good; it is full of joy and gladness. It sustains our very life.

We should try more frequently to desire nothing else than to have him as the support of our life. And let us beg this of him without any lack of faith. Our natural inclination to perishable objects will attract us, I repeat, much more frequently than we should wish. But at least, let us not deliberately and expressly ask for them. Let us rather have no other concern than to address to our Lord the petition I have just spoken of. If it be granted, we shall want for nothing.

The Effect of Holy Communion on the Body

Do you not believe that this most holy food is beneficial nourishment even for the body and a remedy for even physical ailments? Personally, I am sure that it is. I know a person who was afflicted with serious infirmities and who frequently endured the most acute pains. However, when she received communion, she was instantaneously cured of these ills, as though by the touch of one's hand. This favor was granted to her frequently. And what is more, her maladies were so apparent, that I do not see how they could have been pretended ones.

The Marvelous Effects of Eucharist on the Soul

Since the marvels worked by this sacred bread in the souls of those receiving it worthily are so well-known, I am not going to speak of the numerous ones that I could narrate of this particular person. I was in a position to know of them, and I am certain that the person in question is worthy of belief. Our Lord gave her such a lively faith that when she heard people say that they wished they had lived in the time of Christ, our Sovereign Good, she used to smile to herself. For, she thought to herself, what more could we desire, since we possess him in the Most Holy Sacrament just as truly as though we had lived with him then?

Even though this person was not very perfect, I know that for many years, at the moment of holy communion, she beheld our Lord entering the dwelling of her soul, just as clearly as if she had seen him with the eyes of her body. She strove to increase her faith, and believing that our Lord truly entered the abode of her soul, she detached herself from all exterior distractions as well as she could, and entered therein with him. She placed herself, as it were, in a quiet nook, in order to recollect the senses and to dwell alone with her Lord.

She controlled her senses so as to make them perceive the ineffable grace she enjoyed, or rather, to prevent their interfering with the soul in its enjoyment of its God. In spirit, she placed herself at his sacred feet and wept in company with Magdalene, just as though she actually beheld him in the house of the Pharisee. And even though she felt no devotion, her faith assured her that he was truly there.

The Actual Presence of Jesus in the Soul

If we are not hopelessly dull and willfully blinded, we cannot doubt his presence here. It is not a question of the imagination, as it is, for instance, when we picture our Lord on the Cross, or in some other mystery of his passion. At such times, we relive the scene as it happened in the past. But here it is a question of the actual presence of Jesus, and there can be no doubt about this. There is no need to go in search of our Lord elsewhere, at a distance from us, for we know that until the accidents of bread have been consumed by the natural action of the body, the good Jesus is within us. Let us therefore draw near him.

When he was upon earth, the mere contact with his garments healed the sick. If we have faith, why should we doubt that he will not work miracles while he is so intimately united with us? Why should he not grant our petitions, while he is the guest of our soul? His Majesty is not accustomed to repay one poorly in return for gracious hospitality.

If you are disconsolate at not seeing him with your bodily eyes, understand that this would not be expedient for us here. It is one thing to see him as he is in glory, another to behold him as he was in this world. We are such weak human beings on this earth that no one could possibly contemplate him in his glory. As a matter of fact, the world would cease to exist for us in the attempt. In any case, no one would want to return to live in it. A glimpse of the Eternal Truth would reveal to us that everything we value here is nothing but a lie and a mockery. How could a poor sinner like myself, who has offended him so much, approach him after beholding his sublime Majesty? But under the accidents of bread, he is within easy reach to all.

Jesus Hidden in the Eucharist

It would seem that when a king disguises himself, we are not obliged to concern ourselves about court etiquette, its formal rules, and the like in order to converse with him. Moreover, his very purpose in disguising himself seems precisely to be that we omit all ceremony.

And thus it is with our Lord. Otherwise, how could we dare, with such tepidity, unworthiness, and imperfection, to approach him? Alas, how far we are from understanding what we request, and how wonderfully he has arranged all things in his wisdom. When he notices that a soul profits by his presence, he reveals himself to that soul. The one thus favored will not discern our Lord with bodily eyes, but the divine Guest will make himself known either by wonderful interior sentiments or by various other means.

Find your joy in abiding with him. Do not waste the hour after holy communion, which provides you with so favorable an opportunity for acquainting him with your interests. Realize that this time is very precious for the soul. It can profit by these moments to glorify the good Jesus in a wonderful way. Remain in his company. Take special care not to lose him.

Remaining in Spirit with Jesus

If obedience orders you to undertake other tasks, make it a point to remain in spirit with our Lord. He is your Master. Even though you may not perceive it, nevertheless, he will not fail to teach you. But if you straightway direct your thoughts to some other object and pay no more attention to his presence within you than if you had not received him at all, do not blame him, but blame only yourself for your loss.

Lest you be tempted to accuse me of inconsistency, because I seem to be treating here of contemplation, I wish you to understand that I am not telling you to refrain from reciting vocal prayers, unless our Lord should raise you to contemplation. But if you do recite the Our Father, try to realize how truly you are in the company of him who taught you this prayer.

Danger of Distracting Preoccupations

If you immediately become preoccupied with distracting affairs, and give no heed to him who is within you, how can he make himself known to your soul? The time of which I am speaking, namely, immediately after holy communion, is a particularly opportune time. It is then that the Master personally teaches you. Listen to him. Kiss his sacred feet in gratitude for his having deigned to instruct you. Then beg him not to depart from you.

In my opinion, it would be absurd for you to make this petition while gazing on a picture of Christ, because that would be to abandon his holy person in favor of an image of him. Would it not be folly on our part to speak to the portrait of a person, instead of to the person himself when he came to visit us? Do you wish to know when it is profitable to use a picture of our Lord, and when this expedient is a source of joy to me? It is when he is absent or when, by reason of the aridities in which he places us, he would have us think he is not present.

Fervor Aroused by Sacred Images

At such a time, it is a great help to look upon the image of our Blessed Lady or of some saint to whom we have a special devotion, or, better still, of Christ himself, for this rouses the soul to even a greater fervor. As for me, I should like to see his image wherever I turned my eyes. What is better and more pleasing to our gaze than the contemplation of him who loves us so ardently, and who contains in himself all good things? How unfortunate are those heretics who, by their own fault, have lost this consolation as well as many others!

The Habit of Remaining in the Presence of Jesus

Since you possess our Lord in person after holy communion, endeavor to close the eyes of the body, and opening those of the soul, look into your heart. I tell you, and I repeat it, and I should like to say it a thousand times that if you form the habit of remaining in his presence, not only once or twice, but every time you receive holy communion and that if you strive to have such purity of conscience that you may frequently approach the holy table, he will not conceal himself. Rather, in proportion to your desire to contemplate him, he will manifest himself to you in many ways. In fact, he will reveal himself entirely to you, if you bring sufficient love to him.

On the other hand, what can he do if you pay no heed to him, but immediately after receiving him, rudely leave him to pursue commonplace things? Must he force us to gaze upon him in order to fulfill his desire to make himself known to us? Assuredly not! After all, people did not treat him very well when he manifested himself openly to them and declared clearly who he was. And, nevertheless, how pitifully small was the number of those who believed in him!

The Appreciation of the Divine Presence in the Soul

He has granted us an inestimable favor of great mercy in assuring us that he, Infinite Majesty, is present in the Most Holy Sacrament. But to manifest himself openly, to communicate his blessings, and to give his treasures, are favors reserved for bestowal on those who love him ardently. Such persons are his true friends. Whoever is not of this number, and whoever does not do everything possible to prepare worthily for holy communion, should never dare to ask our Lord to manifest himself. Such a one has scarcely fulfilled what the Church prescribes for holy communion when he abandons the interior life of recollection and dismisses God from his soul, and thereupon becomes engrossed in the business, preoccupations, and distractions of worldly life. One would be tempted to say that so careless a person has nothing more urgent to do than, at the earliest possible moment, drive our Lord out from the abode that is really his own.

Chapter Nine

"GIVE US THIS DAY OUR DAILY BREAD" *(concluded)*

Spiritual Communion

I have dwelt upon this point at length here, despite the fact that I had previously referred to it when, in explaining the prayer of recollection, I emphasized the importance of interior recollection in reference to being alone with God.

Whenever you attend Mass and cannot receive holy communion, communicate spiritually. This practice is extremely profitable. Similarly, recollect yourself interiorly. In this way you will foster in yourself a profound love for our Lord. For from the moment you dispose yourselves properly to receive him, he never fails to grant some special favor in his own mysterious way.

Approaching him is like drawing near to a fire. Even if this fire be blazing, it will not warm us very much if we withdraw to a distance, and fail to stretch out our hands to it, though it is true that we shall feel warmer than we should in an unheated room. But this is not what happens when we draw near to our Lord in the eucharist. If the soul is well disposed and sincerely wishes to rid itself of coldness, a few moments in his presence will suffice to enkindle it for several hours.

Perhaps at the beginning, you will not find this practice helpful. That is because the demon, realizing the discomfiture he will suffer as a result, will cause you distress and anguish of heart. He will even put it into your head that you would derive more devotion from other religious practices. But do not abandon this method, for our Lord will discern in it the great love you bear him.

Few Followers of Jesus in Suffering

Remember, there are few souls who accompany him and who follow him on the way of the Cross. Let us, then, be willing to suffer something for him. He will not fail to repay us. Furthermore, let us recall how many souls there are who not only neglect his company, but who even expel him shamefully from their abode. Consequently, to prove our desire to see him, we ought to suffer something for him.

Since he suffers everything and is ready to endure all in order to find one single soul who will welcome and lovingly entertain him, each one of you should strive to be that soul. If there were no souls of such dispositions, his Father, obviously, would not permit him to remain in our midst. But God is such a good Friend to his friends and so kind a Master to his servants that, beholding the ardent love of his well-beloved Son, he permits him to bestow himself in such an excellent work. For there the perfect love of the Son for the Father and for us shines forth in radiant glory.

Pleading the Cause of Jesus

Oh Holy Father, who art in heaven, it is evident that you wish us to possess the boon of your Son's presence, because you can refuse us nothing that will contribute to our happiness. Someone is needed, as I have said, to plead his cause, since he seems to forget his own interests. Why then, oh devoted souls, should we not assume that role, timid as we may be in view of our unworthiness? But let us have confidence. Our Lord commands us to plead. In the spirit of obedience, therefore, let us do so in the name of Jesus.

Let us say to the divine Majesty: Your Beloved Son, in giving us poor sinners the ineffable gift of the holy eucharist, has omitted nothing. In your mercy, do not permit him to be so ignominiously maltreated. Since your Beloved Son has given us such an admirable means of offering him in sacrifice, grant that a single offering of such inestimable value be sufficient to check the course of outrages and acts of irreverence committed in the places where the Most Blessed Sacrament is present. . . .

CHAPTER TEN

"FORGIVE US OUR TRESPASSES, AS WE FORGIVE THOSE WHO TRESPASS AGAINST US"

Meaning of Christian Forgiveness

Our good Master now sees that this heavenly food renders everything easy to accomplishment for us, unless the fault is ours. Hence, we are now very well enabled to accomplish those words addressed to his Father, "Thy will be done in us." And thus he tells his Father to forgive us our trespasses, because we forgive one another. He continues, then, the prayer he is teaching us, and adds the words, "Lord, forgive us our trespasses, as we forgive those who trespass against us."

Notice that he does not say, "As we *shall* forgive." Consequently, we are to understand that whoever requests so great a favor, and who has previously surrendered his will entirely into the hands of God, must of necessity *have forgiven* those who have trespassed against him. That is why our Savior says, "As we forgive those who trespass against us." Hence, whoever has said sincerely, "Thy will be done" must of necessity actually have forgiven already, or at least have firmly resolved to do so.

Notice, then, why the saints rejoiced in the midst of wrongs and persecutions. It gave them something to offer to God when they directed this petition to him. Otherwise, what would a poor soul like my own have to offer, who has so little to forgive, and who is itself in such great need of pardon? We ought seriously to consider this truth. On the simple condition of our forgiving one another, no less a favor is granted us than our Lord's own pardon for sins which should have merited eternal fire. And after all, what really have we to forgive? Not actual wrongs, but only mere trifles that amount to nothing!

Pardon of Wrongs

For what real wrong can one possibly inflict upon a person like me, who deserves to be tormented by the demons for all eternity? If one treats me ill in this world, is this not according to justice? Oh Lord, on this score, I have nothing to offer you in exchange for the pardon which I beg for my offenses. May your divine Son deign to forgive me! No one has really wronged me, and thus I have had nothing to forgive for love of you. But, oh Lord, accept at least my willing dispositions.

I believe that I would be ready to forgive everything, in order to merit your pardon. For the same reason, I would be ready to fulfill your will without any reserve, though I hasten to confess that I do not know with certainty how I should react were someone really to accuse me unjustly. At present, I acknowledge my guilt before you, although everyone else may pass favorable judgment upon me. For my part, I have so little to forgive that you, oh Lord, must pardon me without my having fulfilled the condition you have laid down. This is but another occasion for showing your mercy.

May you be praised, oh heavenly Father, for bearing with me despite my nothingness. Since, however, your Son made this request in the name of all my debts that will be paid even though I come to you empty-handed and totally devoid of resources.

Generous Unconcern About Wrongs and Affronts

But, oh my Lord, are there not other persons like me who have not fully realized this truth? If there are,

I beg them, in your name, to take serious thought, and not to be unduly concerned about certain insignificant wrongs which they call affronts. To be bothered about trifling points of honor is to act like children who would build playhouses out of straw.

Oh great God, why is it that we will not understand in what real honor consists and what its loss entails? It would assuredly be a disaster if you, oh devoted souls of Christ, did not understand this truth. Hence, I do not refer to you at present; I am speaking rather of myself, and of the time when, obsessed with the thought of honor without knowing what it really meant, I drifted along in the fashion of the world with the worldly wise. How thoroughly ashamed I am of all this now, as I think of the things that absorbed me then. And yet, I was not the type of person who usually became unduly engrossed in such things. But neither was I attracted by what is of prime importance; that is to say, I did not understand, nor was I interested in, the honor that is profitable and useful to the soul.

The World's False Judgment of Honors

How truly the person spoke, who said, "Honor and profit do not consort together." I do not know if he was really referring to this subject. Nevertheless, it is literally verified here; for that which benefits the soul is incompatible with worldly honor. It is appalling to behold the perverse tendencies of the world on this score. Blessed be God, who has deigned to take us out of the world! May it please his Majesty to keep the world always as distant from this house as it is now! May God spare us from having monasteries where concern about honor and precedence is the principal preoccupation of the religious! In them, God would not be much honored.

False Notions of Dignities

Nevertheless, oh devoted souls of Christ, realize that Satan does not lose sight of you. He sets up points of honor even in monasteries. In these, just as in the world, he determines the rules by which one rises or falls in dignities. Thus, for instance, learned persons must advance according to their learning. I confess, however, that I do not understand how this custom is observed. If one has advanced to the teaching of theology, he should not lower himself by lecturing in philosophy, because the rules of honor dictate that one must advance and not recede. If obedience, however, imposed it upon him, he would feel wronged, and there would be others, too, who would agree with him and consider this order as an affront. Then Satan in turn would supply them with reasons to prove that the very law of God countenanced their attitude.

The same is true even among nuns. She who has once been prioress is considered no longer eligible for any inferior position. The senior in rank expects marks of respect and never for a moment forgets her standing. Sometimes she even demands these marks of deference as her due, since the rule enjoins them.

The Paramount Importance of Humility

This is enough to make one laugh, if it did not more fittingly provoke tears. Would you, by any chance, say that our rule does not command us to practice humility? Undoubtedly, these regulations are intended to promote good order, but is it for me to insist that I be paid all due marks of deference? Should I be as solicitous about the observance of these points of the rule as I should be about other points, which I probably observe imperfectly? All religious perfection is not bound up in this one point of the rule. Others will keep it carefully, even though I myself am heedless about it.

The fact is that our very nature urges us to ascend, even though this is not how we get to heaven. Human nature does not want to descend. Oh Lord, Lord! Are you not our exemplar and our Master? Surely you are!

But you, who are the very source of all honor, in what did you confide your honor? Certainly you did not lose it in humbling yourself unto death. No, Lord, far from it! You thereby merited honor for all.

For the love of God, oh devoted souls of Christ, be wary of all points of honor and precedence. The very first steps on this pathway lead one astray. God grant that no soul be lost by an attachment to these petty points of precise etiquette, through failure to understand the real nature of true honor. If we forgive some trifle, which was neither an affront, nor a wrong, nor anything of account, we eventually come to believe that we have acted with magnanimity. As a consequence, we shall ask our Lord to forgive us in return for what we led ourselves to believe was forgiveness on our part.

Oh my God, make us realize that we do not really know ourselves, and that we come to you with empty hands. In your infinite mercy, deign to grant us forgiveness. In truth, oh Lord, because on the one hand, everything here is perishable, and on the other, punishment is eternal, I find nothing worthy to present to you that would merit the inestimable favor of your pardon, except the mercy of your divine Son.

The Need of Mutual Forgiveness

Who can express just how pleasing to our Lord must our mutual love be? The good Jesus could have presented other motives to his Father. He could have said, "Forgive us, oh Lord, because of our many penances, prayers, and fasts, or because we have left all things for you, and have loved you exceedingly." But he said nothing of the sort.

Nor did he say, "Forgive us, because we are ready to sacrifice our lives for you." But he only said, "As we also forgive those who trespass against us." Perhaps he said this because, seeing how concerned we are about the petty points of honor, and realizing that nothing is harder for us to trample underfoot, he knows that nothing will be more pleasing to the Father than our renouncement of paltry honors. And so, Jesus made his Father this offering on our behalf.

Resolute Determination to Pardon Others

Notice the expression our Lord employs, "As we forgive those who trespass against us." Here we are concerned, I repeat, with something we have already done. Observe with care whether the soul is resolutely determined to forgive, after having received the graces that God grants in this prayer, which I have called perfect contemplation. Likewise, consider whether the soul actually pardons all wrongs, no matter how grave they may be, when the occasion for forgiveness arises. I do not refer to insignificant trifles that some dignify with the name of wrongs and that do not affect the soul raised by God to this high form of prayer. It matters little whether such a soul is esteemed or not. Rather, to speak more correctly, such a soul is more afflicted by esteem than by contempt, and it suffers more chagrin from overwhelming joy and peace than from toil.

The Heavy Crosses of Contemplatives

When God has really bestowed his kingdom upon anyone here below, that one no longer desires any other kingdom in this world. Such a one realizes that this is the true way to follow, in order to reign in a superior manner. Experience has already shown such a soul the great profit and progress derived from suffering for God. Rarely does God grant such favors except to those souls who have voluntarily suffered the most painful trials for him. As I have previously explained in this book, the crosses of contemplatives are extremely heavy, and our Lord gives them only to souls who have been thoroughly tried.

Contemplatives Seek Crosses

These souls realize perfectly the nothingness of the things of the world, and so attach no great value to transitory matters. They may, it is true, experience a momentary feeling of vexation at some great wrong or severe trial. Immediately, however, reason comes to their aid, and overcomes the feeling of distress. Their chagrin is then completely dispersed by a joy that overwhelms them, when they see that our Lord offers them this opportunity to gain more favors and eternal merits in one day than they could have earned by ten years of self-chosen trials. In my opinion, this is the disposition of soul that is ordinarily theirs. I have conversed with a great number of contemplatives on this matter, and I am certain of it. While others seek gold and precious stones, these souls value and prize only the crosses they know will bring them true riches.

The Genuine Humility of Contemplatives

Such persons are far from indulging in self-esteem. They are happy when their sins are known, and they even reveal them when they discern that they are esteemed. Nor do they boast about their noble ancestry, because they realize that this does not aid them to reach the eternal kingdom. If they should delight in their noble lineage, it would be only because it enabled them to render more glory to God. In any other case, they suffer when they are esteemed more highly than they deserve. Furthermore, they count it a real joy, rather than an abasement, to undeceive those who overrate them. It is certain that the souls to whom God grants this humility and this profound love of his glory so completely forget themselves when it is a question of serving him, that they cannot imagine others being sensitive to, or even mindful of affronts.

The Prayer of Union

These last effects that I will treat are found ordinarily among those who have arrived at a high degree of perfection, and whom our Lord, by drawing them to himself, has raised to perfect contemplation. However, the first effects, which consist in a resolute desire to suffer wrongs and to bear with them despite their painfulness, can be obtained in a short time when one is favored by the prayer of union. If a soul does not obtain these effects, or does not acquire from this prayer a firm resolution to suffer, then it should judge that its prayer is not God given, but rather an illusion, an insidious species of joy sent by Satan with the intention of nourishing self-esteem.

The Generous Forgiveness of Wrongs

It is possible that a beginner in this prayer of union will not have this strength right away. But if God really continues to favor this soul, it will acquire it without delay. Even though the soul may not have great proficiency in the other virtues, at least it will find it easy to be sincere in forgiving those who have inflicted injury upon it. I cannot believe that a soul so intimately united to the Infinite Mercy, wherein it sees its own nothingness and the extent of God's forgiveness, would fail to pardon an offense immediately and most willingly or would fail to experience the most kindly sentiments toward those who had inflicted wrongs. The soul perceives such sublime pledges of love in the graces and favors lavishly bestowed upon it by God that it rejoices in finding an opportunity to give some token of love in return.

Spitefulness Incompatible With High Spirituality

I know many, I repeat, whom our Lord has chosen to raise to these supernatural states, to this prayer of union or of contemplation that I have just described. And though I discerned other faults and imperfections in them, never did I see one who was spiteful. In fact, I believe that a person could not possibly be so, when, as I have said, the favors truly come from God.

The Increase of Divine Favors

The person receiving great favors ought to observe whether these effects continue to increase. If they do not, the person has cause for great fear, and should be told that these supposed favors do not come from God. God always enriches the soul of the one whom he deigns to visit. This is certain; for even though the favor and the joy of these exalted forms of prayer pass quickly, the soul gradually perceives the benefits that accrue from them. Since the good Jesus knows this perfectly, he expressly tells his Father, "And forgive us our trespasses, as we forgive those who trespass against us."

CHAPTER ELEVEN

"FORGIVE US OUR TRESPASSES, AS WE FORGIVE THOSE WHO TRESPASS AGAINST US" *(concluded)*

The Wonderful Perfection of the Our Father

What great perfection there is in this gospel prayer! How truly worthy it is of so good a Master! And what acts of gratitude we should make to God for it! It is so admirably composed that each one can apply it for his own personal advantage. I marvel exceedingly to see how all perfection and contemplation are comprised in so few words. It appears that we have no need to study any other book.

Thus far, our Lord has taught us all the degrees of prayer and of exalted contemplation, from those of ordinary mental prayer to quietude and union. If only I knew how to expound this entire doctrine, I could compose an extended treatise on prayer, based on this solid foundation.

The Universal Nature of the Our Father

Here our Lord begins to make us understand the effects produced by those favors of which I have spoken, when they are truly from him. As you will remember, I asked myself why our Lord did not explain more clearly these profound and difficult points so that all might understand them. It seemed to me that since this prayer was universal and intended for all, it should be possible for every one of us to use it as an expression of his personal wants and to find consolation in the thought that it is so admirably suited to his own individual needs.

Blessed be his name for all ages! Through him, I beg the Eternal Father to forgive me my debts and my enormous sins. As for myself, I have really never had anything to pardon anyone, whereas each day I have fresh need of forgiveness. May he some day grant to me the grace to offer him some sacrifice, so that I can truly say, "Forgive me, as I also forgive."

The Sons of God and Brothers of Jesus

The good Jesus has thus taught us an exalted form of prayer, and has asked his Father that we might be as angels in this exile. We should therefore make every effort to conform our deeds to our words. Briefly, we ought in some way to appear like the sons and daughters of so great a Father, and brothers and sisters of so great a Brother. His Majesty will not fail to grant our requests when he sees that our actions really conform to our words. Our Lord will bestow his kingdom upon us and will grant us the supernatural gifts of the prayer of quiet, of perfect contemplation, and the other favors he is accustomed to lavish upon the soul in this state. He will thus respond to our least efforts; for, after all, whatever we can do of ourselves is extremely insignificant. But no matter what our capability may be, it is certain that the Eternal Father will aid us, because of his Son's prayer in our behalf.

Contemplatives who no longer seek the things of earth, and souls who have given themselves unreservedly to God, may request such heavenly favors as the infinite mercy can accord them here below. Those, however, who, bound by the ties of this world, must live in it according to their state of life, may ask for material bread and the other things needed for their families. For them, such a petition is just and holy.

The Surrender of Self-Will and Forgiveness of Injuries

But notice carefully that there are two things necessary for all, namely, the surrendering of our will to God and the forgiveness of wrongs. It is true, I repeat, that these occur by degrees. Thus, the perfect resign their will to God in a perfect manner and pardon wrongs in the perfect way previously described. We, on our part, should do whatever we can. Our Lord accepts all that is offered him. It *seems* as though our Savior has concluded a sort of contract with his Eternal Father framed in this fashion: "Do this, oh Lord, and my brothers and sisters will do that." It is certain that he will not disregard his promise. Oh, how liberally does he pay! How well he knows how to reward us beyond our due!

Candor and Simplicity

He will enrich us with his gifts from the time he perceives that we recite this prayer perfectly and in a disinterested manner and that we are firmly resolved to transform our words into deeds. Above all, he wants us to approach him with candor, simplicity, and sincerity, and without any mental reservations. Whenever we act in this way, he always gives us much more than we ask for.

The Courage of Valiant Souls

Our good Master knows all this. He sees that those souls who make this petition perfectly will attain to the exalted state through special graces from his Father. He understands that those who have reached or resolutely tend toward perfection are without fear and ought to remain so. He sees that they trample the world underfoot and please him, who is sovereign of the world. Inebriated with these delights, they do not willingly recall that there is any other world or that they still have adversaries to oppose.

Oh eternal Wisdom! Oh devoted Master! What a favor to have a Master who is wise and prudent, and who can anticipate perils. This is the very embodiment of all that a truly spiritual person can desire in this world, since it insures profound security. I am incapable of estimating the value of such a grace.

The Danger of Adversaries and of Illusions

Our Lord sees that it is necessary to keep these souls on the alert and to remind them of their enemies. He knows that it is even more dangerous for them than for others to be off their guard. They have greater need of help from the Eternal Father, since their fall would be from a greater height. Finally, lest they inadvertently become victims of illusion, in their name, he addresses to his Father these petitions so necessary for all of us living in this land of exile, "And lead us not into temptation, but deliver us from evil."

Chapter Twelve

"AND LEAD US NOT INTO TEMPTATION, BUT DELIVER US FROM EVIL"

The Necessity of Trials and Combat

These are exalted favors that we must here consider and understand, because we have to ask them of God. Let us begin by studying one point that I view as absolutely certain. It is this: those who reach perfection do not ask God to be freed from trials, temptations, persecutions, and combat. To be afflicted by trials is but another apparent and unmistakable proof that such souls are guided by the Holy Spirit and that they are not deluded when they view contemplation and other special favors as coming from the hand of

God. And I repeat, these souls prefer trials; they even request and love them.

They are like soldiers hoping for the rewards of battle. The more often they fight, the happier they are. If there is no combat, soldiers have to be content to live on their pay, and they well know that they will never enrich themselves in that fashion.

Conflicts, the Lot of Soldiers of Christ

Believe me, the hour of conflict never comes soon enough for soldiers of Christ; that is, for those who are raised to contemplation and who dedicate themselves to prayer. They never have great fear of their proclaimed adversaries, for they know them and are aware that such opponents have no real power against those armed with the strength of God. They always come forth as victors from the fight, enriched with rewards. Such souls are never put to flight by their enemies.

Demons Are Traitors

It is the traitors whom they have good reason to fear, and against whom they beg protection from our Lord. These latter are the demons who deceitfully transform themselves into angels of light and the enemies who disguise themselves until they have caused the greatest harm to the soul. They do not make known their real identity, but they gradually suck the very lifeblood of the soul and destroy virtue so that we fall into temptation without realizing it. These are the real adversaries from whom we should often beg our Lord to deliver us when we recite the Our Father. Ask him never to permit us to succumb to temptation nor to become victims of illusion. Let us beseech him to show us the poison. May our enemies never hide the light and truth from us. How right our Good Master was in teaching us this petition and addressing it to his Father for us!

The Danger of Delusions

Realize that our hidden enemies can harm us in many ways. Do not think that it is solely by deluding us into believing that the joys and consolations that they may bring come from God. In my opinion, this is the least harm they can cause to souls. As a matter of fact, these joys and consolations may even inspire some to advance in the service of God. These joys may attract such souls to devote more time to prayer. Being ignorant of the influence of Satan over their souls, they unceasingly thank God and feel obliged to serve him ever more fervently, particularly in view of their unworthiness of such favors. They should endeavor to show more fidelity so that our Lord will add new graces to those they suppose themselves to have already received.

Humility, a Protection Against Satan

Strive to be always humble. Realize that you are not worthy of such exalted graces, and do not seek them. I am convinced that in this way, Satan loses many souls he had conceitedly looked upon as already ruined. Thus, from the evil Satan sought to cause, his Majesty draws good. Our Lord sees that our intention, in remaining close to him in prayer, is to please and serve him. And he is always faithful to his promises. Nevertheless, we should be on our guard so as not to offend against humility or give way to vainglory. Beg our Lord to save you from such harm, and do not fear that his Majesty will permit you for long to receive consolations from anyone but himself.

The Danger of Imaginary Virtues

Unknown to ourselves, Satan may cause great harm by deluding us into the belief that we have virtues which in reality we do not possess. This is a real evil. Through heedlessness we take a path that appears safe, and straightway we fall into a quagmire from which we cannot free ourselves. If we do not commit a mortal sin that drags us to hell, at least our feet are fettered and we cannot follow the way of perfection.

How can one walk when he has fallen into a deep marsh? He is doomed to finish his days there. He will be fortunate if he does not go deeper and fall into hell. In all events, he will never make progress. If such misfortune is his state, he will be of no help to himself or to others. In fact, he would be harmful to them, for since the pit is already there, many who pass by the way can fall into it. But if the one sunk in the bog climbs out and fills the pit with soil, no further harm will come to him or to others.

I warn you then that the temptation by which the demon deludes us, causing us to think that we have virtues we do not really possess, is a very dangerous one. I know this full well from experience. I can speak on this subject, although not so well as I should wish.

The Deceits of Satan

Satan, for example, gives you to understand that you are poor. There is some truth in this, since you have made a vow of poverty to God, at least with the lips. He has even convinced prayerful persons of this. I have said, "with the lips," because it is impossible that Satan should keep us ensnared by this temptation for twenty years and even for a lifetime, if we fully realized what we promised and had made this promise with heartfelt sincerity. Surely we should see that by such conduct, we mislead the world and deceive ourselves.

The Need for Genuine Poverty

We have made the promise of poverty. Or at least, we who believe ourselves poor say, "I do not desire any of the goods of this world, but I am keeping this object because it is essential, and I must live to serve God. After all, he wishes us to nourish our body." And thus we must offer deceitful excuses for a thousand different things, which the demon, disguised as an angel of light, represents as reasonable. He persuades us that we are already poor and that since we really possess the virtue of poverty, we need not strive further to acquire it.

We cannot discover whether or not we have the virtue unless we examine our actions attentively. One who has an excessive interest in temporal things will not be slow to show it. However, a person who is truly poor has so little esteem for the goods of this world that he is never disquieted when, for one legitimate motive or another, he has to seek them. If he lacks something, he gives no further thought to it; if he becomes truly poor, he is not much preoccupied with his poverty. Earthly goods are for him not a primary concern, but only a secondary one. His thoughts are more exalted.

The Danger of Superfluities

Religious who are poor do not own anything, because at times they really have nothing to possess. But should someone give them something, rarely would they consider it superfluous. They are always happy to have something in reserve. If they can have a garment of finer cloth, they will not ask for cloth of coarser texture. They desire to possess a multiplicity of things, even though it be only a small reserve of funds to insure their needs should illness require more than ordinary care.

Have you not promised God that you will not be preoccupied about the things of the world, and no matter what might happen, to abandon yourselves without reserve to his providence? But if you are constantly concerned lest you lack something, would it not be preferable to have fixed revenues, as a means of avoiding anxieties?

Furthermore, even though we may possess such revenues without sin, it is well for us to understand the imperfections we commit against poverty so that we may see how far we are from possessing this virtue. And we ought to ask God for this poverty and strive to acquire it. For if we erroneously believe that we already have it, we shall pass up all opportunities to acquire it. And what is worse, we are living under an illusion.

Genuine Humility

The same is true of the virtue of humility. It may appear that we do not seek the esteem of persons and that we are detached from everything. But when we are put to the test, very soon our resentment and our actions manifest that we are not humble. Nor do we spurn the little esteem that we receive. In a similar fashion, the poor of whom I just spoke do not refuse an object that can be of some slight advantage to them. And still God wills that they not seek anything for themselves!

Consolations from God

When we receive joys and consolations from God, we feel that we on our part do nothing but accept these gifts from him. Hence, we feel that we should serve God with greater fidelity in gratitude for them. On the other hand, when consolations come from Satan, we seem to think that we are the ones proffering the gifts to God, and that we are rendering him a service that he must repay. And by these deceitful notions, Satan gradually works the greatest harm in the soul. On the one hand, he weakens humility, while on the other, he makes us negligent in the acquiring of a virtue we mistakenly think we possess.

Deceitful Consolations from Satan

What remedy have we against this temptation? The best seems to be the one our Master gives us. He tells us to pray and to beg the Eternal Father not to permit us to fall into temptation. But I would suggest an additional remedy. If our Lord seems to have given you some particular virtue, consider it as a loan that he can withdraw at will. And this really often happens, though not without his special providence. I know this from personal experience. Sometimes I feel that I am very much detached from the things of the world, and at times I prove that I am. But on the contrary, at other times I find myself so attached to certain things—things that perhaps I should have laughed at on the preceding day—that I can hardly recognize myself.

The Vacillating Character of Human Beings

One day I feel that I have great courage and that were it a matter of God's service, I would not recoil before any obstacle, and on certain days I have proved this. Nevertheless, on the next day, I do not have the courage to kill an ant, for the love of God, even though I have the least possible difficulty in doing so. Again, at times I feel that I would be insensible to every kind of slander and calumny, and on several occasions I have proved the existence of such sentiments, and have even experienced joy in the trials. Nevertheless, there are days when a single word afflicts me, and I long to leave this world, because everything wearies me. I am not the only person disturbed by such vacillations of temperament. I have verified this with certainty in persons much better than myself.

Docile Dependence Upon God

Since this is so, who among us can claim for ourselves virtue or a wealth of virtues? At the very times we need these virtues most, we find ourselves absolutely destitute. On the contrary, let us consider ourselves as truly poor, and let us not contract debts we cannot pay. Our treasure must come from another source. We never know when our Lord will leave us in the prison of our misery without aid from him. If others consider us virtuous or if they esteem and respect us, it is merely because of the virtues loaned to us. But if God should withdraw his hand, we and our admirers would become objects of ridicule. Undoubtedly, if we serve God in all humility, he will aid us in our needs. However, if this virtue is not deeply embedded in our souls, our Lord will desert us at every step. In his way, he will show us how much he wants us to work to acquire humility as well as his desire that we possess nothing except what we receive from him.

Dangerous Delusions from Satan

Here is another counsel I would offer you. Satan deceives us into believing that we possess some virtue, for example, patience, because we make a resolution to suffer much for God and also frequently express this desire. We fancy that we would really suffer everything for his glory. We are elated over such dispositions, and Satan, for his part, does not fail to attempt to persuade us that we actually possess them. However, do not place any faith in such virtues. Until they have been put to the actual test, do not think that you know even their name, much less that you have received them from God. For it will happen that even one single annoying word will suffice to exhaust your splendid store of patience.

When you have much to suffer, thank God that he has begun to teach you this virtue of patience and store up courage for further trials. Suffering is an indication that God wishes you to repay him, for he has given you patience that you might exercise it and might look upon it as a loan that can be recalled any time he wishes.

Imaginary Poverty

Another deceitful form of temptation lies in the ruse of Satan to delude us into thinking that we are very poor in spirit. As a matter of fact, we are accustomed to say that we desire nothing and are concerned about nothing. But no sooner does a friend give us something that may not even be necessary, than our entire spirit of poverty vanishes. Since we have formed the habit of saying that we are poor in spirit, we finish by convincing ourselves, though without foundation, that we really are in fact.

Watchfulness Against Illusions

It is very important that we be on our guard to detect and realize the nature of this temptation, whether it concerns the virtues of which I have spoken or a number of others. When our Lord bestows upon us one truly solid virtue, it appears to bring all the others in its train. This is a well-known fact. But I would warn you again always to dread illusions, even when you believe you possess only one virtue. A person who is truly humble is always doubtful of his virtues. He feels that the virtues of others are more genuine and solid than his own.

CHAPTER THIRTEEN

"AND LEAD US NOT INTO TEMPTATION . . ." *(continued)*

The Danger of Discouragement About Past Sins

Let us be on our guard against a certain type of false humility that Satan suggests to us. He seeks to cast us into a state of anguish about the gravity of our sins. This is one point over which he disturbs souls in different ways. He even goes so far as to persuade them, on the plea of their unworthiness, not to receive holy communion and in particular not to pray. If they approach the sacred table to receive holy communion, they wonder whether or not they are well prepared, and in this way they waste the time that should have been employed in drawing fruit from their graces. The anguish of these souls is so great at times, that they imagine that God has abandoned them because of their unworthiness. They almost doubt his mercy. Everything seems full of danger. Their good works, excellent though they be in themselves, they consider useless. Discouragement so enfeebles them that they consider themselves incapable of any good, because they fancy that all that is praiseworthy in others is evil in them.

The Disquieting Effect of False Humility

Consider attentively what I am about to say. It sometimes happens that a profound conviction of your own misery may be an act of humility and genuine virtue. At other times, however, this conviction may be a very subtle temptation. I know, because I have passed through this state. Genuine humility, no matter how profound it may be, never disquiets, never disturbs the soul. Rather it is accompanied by peace, joy, and calm.

The Difference Between Genuine and False Humility

Undoubtedly, the sight of its misery afflicts the soul and clearly shows it that it merits hell. It feels, too, that in justice, all people should abhor it; and so it scarcely dares to beg for mercy. But when humility is genuine, this pain fills the soul with such sweetness and joy that we would gladly be without it. Genuine humility does not distress, nor does it contract the soul; on the contrary, it expands the soul and renders it more capable of serving God. Such is not the effect of false humility. This latter troubles and distresses the soul, and completely upsets it in every way. It likewise fills one with bitterness. In my opinion, Satan's ruse is to destroy our confidence in God by making us believe that we have humility.

We should value humility when it brings us the knowledge of our lowliness, accompanied, nevertheless, by true peace, joy, and consolation. If, on the contrary, the sense of our wretchedness troubles, disquiets, and contracts the soul, and hinders the intelligence from finding true peace, look upon it as a temptation of Satan. Do not, in that case, consider yourselves as genuinely humble. Such humility does not come from God.

Thoughts of the Mercy of God During Trials

When you find yourself under such a trial, divert your thoughts as quickly as possible from the consideration of your own wretchedness. Fix your attention on the mercy of God, on the love which he bears us, and on the sufferings he has endured for us. If there is a real temptation, perhaps you may not succeed in doing this, for Satan will not leave your spirit in peace, but will bother you with things designed to weary you even more. In fact, it will indeed be a great deal if you even recognize such a state as a temptation.

The Danger of Excessive Penances

Similarly, Satan seeks to urge us on to excessive penances. His intention here is to have us consider ourselves more mortified than others, and in this way to convince us that we are doing something. But if you do give yourself up to penitential practices without the knowledge of your confessor of superior, or if you do not discontinue them when they bid you to, then be sure that you have succumbed to temptation. Strive rather to obey, no matter what it costs you, for it is in obedience that the highest perfection consists. And thus we should reason in all our undertakings.

False Sense of Security

Another very treacherous temptation of Satan is a false sense of security. It consists in a certain confident conviction that we could never return to our former faults or to worldly pleasures. We seem convinced of the nothingness of the world, and of its fleeting character, and we imagine that our sole delight is the service of God. This temptation is particularly dangerous when it appears at the beginning of the spiritual life, because the soul, blinded by this sense of security, takes no precautions against the occasions of sin and so succumbs to them. God grant that this second fall be not worse than the first! Because Satan recognizes the harm this soul can do him and the use it can be to others, he loses no opportunity to effectively frustrate its efforts to regain its former meritorious state. Never permit yourselves, then, no matter what consolations and pledges of love you may have received from our Lord, to be lulled into such a false sense of security that you will not fear relapses into sin. Always be on your guard against dangerous occasions of sin.

Genuine Candor With Spiritual Director

Do not fail to make your spiritual favors and consolations known to someone who is capable of guiding you. Conceal nothing from him; for it is precisely here that Satan is wont to work havoc in many ways.

A Humble Spirit of Prayer

However sublime your contemplation may be, make it a point to begin and end your prayer with the realization of your nothingness. Continue always to walk in fear. If your prayer is from God, you will very often, in spite of yourself, reflect upon your own unworthiness, and you will have no need of this counsel. Such prayer engenders humility and always gives us greater light to perceive our nothingness. I shall not insist further, as you can consult many books on this matter. I have spoken about it because I have personally encountered these temptations and have often suffered great anguish from them. I merely add that nothing that one might say is sufficient to insure us complete security.

The Need for Constant Protection Against the Wiles of Satan

Oh Eternal Father, since things are so, what can we do but have recourse to you and beg you not to permit our enemies to lead us into temptations? If only they would attack us openly! Then we could more easily free ourselves with your help. But, who, oh my God, will unmask their secret schemes? We have constant need of your protection. Speak, oh Lord, some word that will enlighten and assure us. You know full well that those who travel the way of prayer are not numerous. And there will be even fewer if, as one attempts to advance, one is beset with so many fears.

Sinners Under the Dominion of Satan

It is indeed a curious fact that the world seems to think that Satan never tempts those who fail to follow the way of prayer. Hence, it is more astounding to see one single soul, though striving for perfection, fall into some illusion, than it is to view a hundred thousand other persons living publicly in sin and deceived by Satan. It requires little effort to determine whether these latter are in a good or bad state, for one can clearly see at a thousand miles away that they are under the domination of Satan.

Astonishment Caused by the Fall of a Prayerful Soul

In truth, the world is right to manifest this astonishment. After all, it has reason to be surprised and to consider it as something novel and rare when Satan does succeed in ensnaring a soul that recites with fervor the Our Father. Usually, one pays little heed to ordinary happenings, but one is astounded by rare and exceptional incidents. That is why the demons themselves encourage this surprise in the worldly minded, for Satan finds that this astonishment works to his advantage, whereas a single soul reaching perfection deprives him of many others.

Protection Assured to Prayerful Souls

I am in no way surprised that the world is amazed at these falls, for such illusions are rare. If a person follows the way of prayer and remains even moderately watchful, such a one is incomparably safer than those following another way. Such a person is like a spectator seated in the elevated balcony at a bullfight, for he is far better protected than those risking the perils of the animal's horns in the arena. This comparison, which I have heard, seems to be literally exact.

Do not fear to follow the ways of prayer. They are numerous. Some find profit in one way, as I have explained, others, in another. But the course is a safe one. You will be freed more readily from temptation by being near our Lord than by remaining at a distance. Beg him, entreat him, to grant you this grace as you repeatedly do each day in reciting the Our Father.

CHAPTER FOURTEEN

"AND LEAD US NOT INTO TEMPTATION . . ." *(continued)*

The Gifts of Love and of Fear

Oh good Master, deign to give us something that will enable us to live without torment in the midst of such dangerous encounters! His Majesty puts a gift at our disposal, the gifts of love and fear. Love will quicken our pace; fear will make us careful on this our journey, which is so beset with dangers. Certainly if we use this gift, we shall not become victims of illusion.

Signs Indicating the Presence of Virtues

Perhaps you will ask me: by what sign can we know that we really possess these two virtues of such great worth? You are right in seeking a sign, for you know that we shall never have an absolutely sure and infallible proof. If we had the assurance that we possessed charity, we should also be certain that we were in the state of grace. Nevertheless, there are some indications of the presence of these virtues that are so obvious that even the blind can see them. And these signs manifest themselves with such persistence and emphasis that one has no choice but to take notice of them. They are the more noticeable because there are so few persons who possess them in all their perfection.

Can one imagine anything greater than the love and fear of God? They are like two fortresses from which the soul sallies forth to wage war on the world and the demons. Those who truly love God love all that is good, favor all that is good, praise all that is good, and cooperate in the support and defense of the good. In a word, they love nothing else but the good and the true, that which is worthy to be loved.

The Incompatibility of the Love of God and the Vanities of World

Do you think it is possible for one who truly loves God to love vanities at the same time? Can you imagine such a one doing that? Of course not! For he who loves God loves neither riches, nor the pleasures of this world, nor its honors. He has a horror of disputes and envy. His sole ambition is to please the Beloved. His longing to be loved by God exhausts his whole strength and spurs him to spend his life in seeking means of pleasing him better. Now how could such love of God be completely hidden? True love can never be concealed.

St. Paul and St. Mary Magdalene

Consider the examples of St. Paul and St. Mary Magdalene. After three days, St. Paul began to show signs that he languished from love (Acts 9:19) as St. Mary Magdalene did from the very first day. Surely their love was evident enough! Undoubtedly, there are degrees of love, and according to its intensity, love manifests itself more or less clearly. But whether feeble or strong, if it is genuinely true love, it shows itself outwardly.

Ardent Love of Contemplatives

Since we are speaking of contemplatives who are exposed to the snares and deceits of Satan, I would add that their love is not feeble. On the contrary, it is always extremely ardent, for they would not be true contemplatives unless it were. This love manifests itself openly and in many ways. It is a most vehement fire, and hence it must burn brightly. If it does not glow thus, the contemplative should distrust herself and realize that she has serious reason to fear. She should endeavor to discover what is wrong and pray and beg our Lord to protect her from falling into temptation.

Perfect Candor With a Confessor

In fact, if a contemplative did not possess this sign of special love, I should fear that she had fallen into temptation. But I repeat, if she is genuinely humble and seeks to know her true condition by opening her soul to a confessor with perfect candor and docility, in spite of all the flattering deceits of Satan, she will receive life instead of the spiritual death the demon so conceitedly planned for her.

Docility as Protection Against Satan

Our Lord is faithful to his promises. Rest assured that if your intention is upright, and you experience no sentiments of pride, what Satan intended for your destruction will give you life. Only be docile to the teachings of the Church, and you need not fear the illusions and deceptions of Satan. Your love of God will not be slow in manifesting itself anew.

Satan's Desire to Disquiet Souls

You may rejoice and be at peace if you experience the love of God, which I have described, and the fear that I am now going to discuss. Satan would like to disquiet you and prevent your enjoying favors so sublime. This is why, either personally or through others, he attempts to arouse vain fears. Since he cannot win you to his cause, he tries at least to deprive you of something. Thus he seeks to harm souls who desire to advance rapidly, and who would really do so if they would but realize that God is the One who actually grants extraordinary graces and that he can likewise richly endow with his gifts such unworthy creatures as we are. At times, we even seem to go so far as to be unmindful of his great mercies in the past.

Satan's Method of Disquieting Souls

Do you think it matters little to Satan to be able to fill us with fear? No indeed! Quite on the contrary, it is of considerable importance to him, because through it he harms us particularly in two ways. First, he terrifies those souls who have heard about the illusions of contemplatives, by making them believe that they likewise would be victims of deception. Secondly, he diminishes the number of those who desire to draw closer to God and who would actually do so if they only realized the immensity of his goodness, which can communicate itself in such an intimate way to poor sinners like us.

The Helpfulness of Knowledge of the Divine Goodness

Certainly the knowledge of such divine goodness would arouse in them, and rightly, a longing for a share in these great favors. Personally, I know several persons encouraged by this consideration. They devoted themselves to prayer, and in a short time they attained to contemplation and received special graces. Hence, oh devoted friends of Christ, thank our Lord fervently when you see one of your own thus favored by him. But do not think that such a sister enjoys complete security. Aid her by praying all the more for her; for no one, surrounded by the perils of this tempestuous sea, can be secure while living on this earth.

Manifestations of Genuine Love

You cannot then fail to recognize this love, wherever it may exist. In fact, I cannot understand how it could possibly be concealed. They say the love that one creature bears toward another cannot be concealed, and still so inferior is this love that it hardly merits the name love, because it is founded on mere nothingness. How then could this other love, so ardent and transcendent, remain effectively hidden? Notice on the one hand, how it constantly goes on increasing, for nothing can hinder it, and on the other, how it rests on the intimate certainty that it is repaid by a like unfailing love. Was not this unfailing love proved by an incomparable manifestation, that is, by the endurance of all forms of sorrows and trials, by the shedding of blood and finally by the surest proof of all, namely, the sacrifice of life?

Final Reliance on Divine Love

Oh great God! What a vast difference the soul that has tried both loves must see between the two! May his Majesty, before he takes us from this life, deign to bestow on us his divine love. For it will be an ineffable source of assurance to us at the hour of death to realize that we are going to be judged by him whom we have loved above all else. Convinced that our debts are paid, we shall be filled with confidence when we appear before his judgment seat. We shall not be going to a foreign country, but to our home, where he whom we love so ardently resides, he who bears us such great love.

The Terrible Lot of Lost Souls

Consider now the great benefits of this love, but realize, at the same time, what an irreparable loss it is to be deprived of it. In that case, the soul would be handed over to the tormentor, delivered into those hands so cruel and hostile to all good, and so partial to all evil. What a terrible fate for the poor soul who, after passing through the pains and dreadful anguish of death, falls immediately into the hands of Satan! And what a frightful form of repose it will find in that abode where it enters! See how it is torn to pieces as it sinks into hell. What a brood of loathsome serpents of every kind! What an appalling place! What must be the feelings of this unfortunate soul! What a terrible abode for the devotees of bodily comfort, who find it indeed a torture to spend a single night in a miserable inn! And yet these are the very ones destined to inhabit hell. What will they think of the lodgings of hell where they must remain throughout all eternity?

The Beginning of the Life of Glory and Avoidance of Purgatory

Seek not the joys of this world. We are well enough off here. After all, we must spend but a single night in an uncomfortable inn. Let us praise God and force ourselves to do penance in this life. How comforting death will be to the person who will escape purgatory, because he will have already made reparation for all his sins! Even here on earth he can begin to enjoy the life of glory, for he can live in perfect peace without any reason for fear.

The Sufferings of Purgatory

Perhaps we shall not reach this state. If we must suffer pain after death, let us beg God to place us in that abode where the hope of final deliverance may aid us to endure our sufferings willingly, and where we shall forfeit neither his friendship nor his grace. Entreat him also to grant us in this life the grace never blindly to enter into an occasion of temptation.

CHAPTER FIFTEEN

"AND LEAD US NOT INTO TEMPTATION . . ." *(concluded)*

The Great Grace of Love of God

At what length have I dwelt upon this subject! And still I have not said as much as I would have wished. If it is so pleasant to speak of divine love, what must it be to possess it? Oh Lord, in your infinite mercy deign to grant me this grace!

The Complete Detachment From the World

Do not permit me to depart from this life until I am absolutely detached from all earthly things, nor before I realize the utter folly of loving anything but you. May I never fall into the error of applying the term *love* to anything in this world! If the foundation is unstable, the building cannot long stand.

The Folly of Seeking Love in This World

I do not understand why we should be surprised when we hear people say, "This person has treated me shamefully; that person does not love me." I merely smile at such foolish remarks! After all, who is bound to repay us? Why should anyone love us? Let these reflections teach you what the world really is. You are tortured by the very love you bear it; this is what crushes you, for your heart bitterly resents your having squandered its affection in child's play.

The Fear of God

Let us now consider the fear of God. But at the outset, I must tell you that I regret being unable here to speak about the love of this world, even though, in punishment for my sins, I was given to know it only too well. Although I should like to make you understand what it is, so you would always keep yourselves from it, I must omit speaking of it so as not to digress from the subject of fear.

The fear of God is also a virtue that is easily perceived by the one possessing it, as well as by one's companions. It is true that at the beginning, this virtue is not perfectly developed, except in those individuals whom God has specially favored and enriched in a short time with many graces. Notwithstanding, this holy fear is always recognized even in beginners. Little by little it grows, and with each succeeding day, this virtue of fear becomes stronger. Then it is not tardy in manifesting itself. You will notice that a soul possessing this fear of God immediately avoids not only sin, but even its occasions as well as bad companions. There are also many other ways by which this fear manifests its presence in a soul.

The Dread of Sin

When the soul has reached contemplation, the fear of God that animates it is very evident. It is to such a soul that I now refer. This virtue, like love, cannot remain hidden in the heart. No matter how closely you observe such persons, you will never find them lacking in recollection. Our Lord shields them so carefully that they would not commit one deliberate venial sin for all the gold in the world. And as for mortal sins, they dread them as they dread fire.

The Fear of Offending God

My wish is that you possess a profound dread of any illusions that may beset you in this matter. Constantly beg our Lord never to permit a temptation to become so violent that it would lead you to offend him, but beg him always to conform it to the strength he has given you, with which to resist it. If you keep your conscience pure, the temptation will cause you little or no harm. It will even redound to your advantage. It is important to keep this point in mind. Such is the fear, then, that I hope you will always retain. It will be your safeguard.

Oh, what a wonderful thing it is, not to have offended God. It is the fear of offending him that enables us to hold in fetters the demons and slaves of hell, for whether they desire or not, all creatures must obey God. The difference between the slaves of hell and us is that they must serve him without choice, whereas we serve God out of love. If we remain pleasing to our Lord, we shall keep the demons at a distance. Despite all their temptations, lies, and cunning, they can do nothing against us that cannot be turned to our advantage.

The Dread of Mortal Sin

Take care, then, to keep your conscience pure. This is a precaution of the greatest importance. Continue striving until you are so resolutely determined never to offend God that rather than commit a single mortal sin, you would be ready to lose a thousand lives and to be persecuted by the entire world.

The Avoidance of Deliberate Venial Sin

You must be equally determined, likewise, to be ever on your guard so as not to commit a deliberate venial sin. I purposely refer to deliberate venial sin, for who does not commit indeliberate ones in great number? There is one form of attentiveness accompanied by deliberation, and there is another that is so sudden that the committing of the fault and our consciousness of it occur in the same instant. In such a case, we have not the opportunity to reflect upon what we do.

Gravity of Deliberate Venial Sin

May God preserve us from all deliberate venial sins, no matter how slight they may appear. I cannot understand how we can have the boldness to oppose so great a God, even though it be in the smallest things. Understand, above all, that it can never be a small matter to offend his divine Majesty, especially when we realize that his loving gaze is fixed on us. In my opinion, a sin which is committed with the consciousness of God's gaze upon us is a completely deliberate sin. It is as if we said, "Lord, I intend to commit this sin, despite your displeasure. I fully realize that you see me, and I know that you will me not to commit this sin. Of all this I am fully conscious.

Nevertheless, I prefer to follow my will and natural tendencies, rather than your will." Can such an offense be a trivial matter? I do not think so. However slight the fault may be in itself, in view of the deliberation which accompanies it, it is great, and even very great.

For the love of God never be negligent on this point. Continue in your present good dispositions. Realize that it is extremely important to accustom yourselves to continue in the spirit of fear, and to understand the significance and gravity of an offense against God. Strive to deepen this conviction and maintain this spirit until the fear of God is embedded little by little in your hearts. It is a question of your very life and even more.

Watchfulness Over Self

Until you are completely convinced that you possess this virtue, you should exercise a great, and even a very great, watchfulness over yourselves. And you ought to avoid all occasions and companions that do not draw you closer to God. Strive earnestly in all your actions and words to conquer your self-will. Avoid saying anything that would not edify others; avoid all conversations that are not of God.

Resolute Striving for Perfection

Much must be done to implant this holy fear of God deeply in the soul. But we shall acquire it much sooner if we are inflamed with true love, and especially if we have the resolute determination never to commit the slightest offense against God. We ought to be willing to endure a thousand deaths, just to avoid one single venial sin. Doubtlessly, we shall fall from time to time, for after all, we are lamentably weak. We ought, as a result, ever to be mistrustful of ourselves. And the firmer our resolutions are, the less we ought to trust ourselves. Our entire confidence must rest in God alone.

The Advantage of a Holy Liberty

When you realize that you possess these dispositions of which I have just spoken, it is no longer necessary to be constrained and timid. Our Lord will strengthen you and your good habits will keep you from offending him. Act now with holy liberty in your lawful dealings with others, even with the worldly. Such people cannot harm you, now that you have a supreme horror of sin. On the contrary, they will incite you to deepen your resolutions still more, inasmuch as they show you what a difference there is between good and evil. If before you possessed the true fear of

God, these persons were a danger to your soul and a source of spiritual death, they will now inspire you to love and praise God all the more for having snatched you from such manifest danger. Formerly, you may have encouraged them in their weaknesses; now you can rescue them by your very presence. Even though they may have no intention of honoring you, your presence will influence them for the better.

The Beneficent Influence of Holy Persons

I often praise God when I reflect upon the source of this beneficent influence. Very frequently, a true servant of God, without speaking a word, can silence blasphemies merely by his presence. The same thing happens in the world. One always respects a friend of ours in our presence; and even though the person be absent, no one will criticize him, simply because he is known to be our friend.

A person in the state of grace has a like influence. The state of grace itself causes the person to be respected, however humble his condition may be. People will avoid causing him distress when they observe how pained he is by an offense against God. I do not understand the precise reason for this, but I know that this is usually the case.

Avoidance of Undue Constraint

Avoid undue constraint in your conduct. When a soul begins to be excessively restrained, it finds itself restricted in all sorts of ways. Sometimes it becomes a prey of scruples and consequently becomes useless to itself and to others. But even if it does not go that far, it will not lead many souls to God, though it work for its own personal sanctification. Human nature is so constituted that the very sight of restraint and stiffness will frighten and repel others from following the way that you pursue, even though it may appear more conducive to virtue. Rather than risk the danger of such constraint, a person will give up the idea of seriously cultivating virtue.

The Danger of Uncharitable Judgments

Another danger arises from this. There will be a tendency to judge others unfavorably, even though they be holier, because they follow a different way than you do. If they act freely and without constraint, in an effort to be helpful to others, you immediately judge them to be imperfect. If you see them give themselves up to holy joy, you consider them dissipated. This is particularly the tendency of pious women who, for want of learning, do not know how to deal with people without committing faults. This is very dangerous, for it is a source of continual and vexing temptations as well as an injury to one's neighbor. Briefly, it is extremely blameworthy to think that those who are less constrained than ourselves are not as perfect as we are.

Undue Timidity

There is still another difficulty. In certain circumstances, when you talk with others or when you are obliged to deal with them, you will be timid about doing so through fear of not being sufficiently reserved on some points. And so, perhaps, you may even commend that which you should have disapproved.

The Importance of Affability

Strive to be affable in so far as you are able without offending God. Deal with all persons in such a way that they will enjoy your conversation and will even wish to imitate your life and manners. Then they will not be terrified by virtue or prejudiced against it. This counsel is extremely important for nuns. The more saintly they are, the more gracious they should be with their sisters. If you sincerely wish to be helpful and acceptable to others, never leave their company, even though their conversation may be unpleasant and may cause you vexation. Strive earnestly to be affable and agreeable. Aim to please all the persons who deal with you, and particularly your sisters.

The Danger of Narrowness of Vision

Understand very clearly that contrary to what you may think, God does not concern himself with such trivial matters. Protect your soul and your spirit from scruples, otherwise you will suffer great loss. Let your intention be upright and your will resolutely determined never to offend God. Do not constrain your soul; for instead of inspiring it to sanctity, you will multiply imperfections into which Satan will lure you. Nor, as I have said, will you be as helpful to yourself or others, as you might have been.

The Confident Trust in God

You understand now how with these two virtues of love and fear of God, we can follow the way of perfection with calm and peace. Therefore, do not look for pitfalls at your every step; if you do, you will never attain to perfection. Since, however, we can never be absolutely sure that we possess these two essential virtues, we should always be on the alert. Fear, consequently, should always be in the vanguard. As long as we remain on earth, we shall never have complete assurance; for that matter, it would even be dangerous for us. It was because he knew this that our Lord, filled with compassion at the sight of a life of uncertainties, temptations, and dangers, has appropriately taught us to beg, as he himself prayed, to be "delivered from evil."

CHAPTER SIXTEEN

"BUT DELIVER US FROM EVIL. AMEN."

Jesus' Weariness of Life

It appears to me that the loving Jesus had good reason to make this petition for himself. We know how weary he was of this life, for at the Last Supper he said to his apostles, "I have ardently desired to eat this Passover with you before I suffer" (Lk 22:15). Since this was his last supper here on earth, we can well surmise how burdensome life had been to him. But now we find people a hundred years old who, instead of being weary of life, yearn to remain on earth as long as possible.

The Sufferings of Christ's Life

We are far, it is true, from experiencing in any way the sufferings, pains, and poverty his Majesty endured.

What was his entire life but a cross, inasmuch as the spectacle of our ingratitude was constantly before him? What was his life but a continual dying, since he had ever before him the dreadful crucifixion he was to undergo? Nevertheless, this was the least of his sorrows. What must he have suffered when he saw the countless offenses committed against his Father and the multitude of souls who would be eternally lost. If such a spectacle causes indescribable torments to a soul filled with the love of God, what torture must it have inflicted on him who is boundless and infinite Love! Rightly then could he plead with his Father to deliver him from such evils and sufferings, and to bestow upon him the eternal peace of the kingdom, of which he is the rightful heir.

Deliverance from All Evils

The amen terminating the Our Father signifies, I believe, that our Lord requests that we, like him, be delivered from all evils forever. But let us not imagine that we can ever be free from numberless temptations, imperfections, or even sins; for "if we say that we have no sin, we deceive ourselves, and the truth is not in us" (1 Jn 1:8). And as to bodily ills and sufferings, who is there that does not experience them in one form or another? Moreover, it is not right to request that we be exempt from these.

Since it seems impossible to be freed from all evils, whether these be ills of body or imperfections, or even faults in the service of God, let us try to understand exactly what we pray for. I do not refer to the saints who, like St. Paul, can do all things in Christ (Phil 4:3), but to a poor sinner like myself. I find myself beset by such weakness, tepidity, lack of mortification and of virtue that I have only one alternative, namely, to beg our Lord to grant some remedy.

Escape From Trials of Life

Request whatever remedy you like. As for myself, I can find none on this earth. That is precisely why I beg our Lord to free me forever from all evil. What good can we find here, where we do not possess the infinite good and where we are so distant from him? Deliver me, oh Lord, from this shadow of death; deliver me from the many toils of life; deliver me from its innumerable sufferings; deliver me from the countless vicissitudes of life; deliver me from the hollow forms of politeness we must employ in this world; deliver me from the endless things that tire and weary me. There are so many of these, that were I to enumerate them, I would unduly bore anyone who should read the list. This weariness must be due to the fact that I have lived *so* wickedly and that even now, in spite of all I owe to God, I am far from living as I should.

Longing for Heaven

I beg our Lord, then, to deliver me forever from all evil. Far from fulfilling the obligations contracted, I perhaps become more indebted to him each day. My real cross, oh Lord, is that I cannot know with certainty whether I love you and whether my desires are pleasing to you. Oh my Lord and my God, deliver me at last from all evil and deign to lead me to the haven of all good. What can they expect here below, they whom you have really enlightened as to this world and whose lively faith has shown them what the Eternal Father has reserved for them? Has not his divine Son requested these things for us, and does he not teach us to beg for them ourselves? Believe me, it is not expedient for us to remain on earth; let us rather desire to be delivered from all evil.

When contemplative souls make this petition with an ardent desire and resolute determination, they have good reason to believe that the graces lavished upon them in prayer come from God. Those who enjoy this favor ought to value highly this desire to leave the world. However, when I yearn for my heavenly home, I do so for another reason. It is because remembering my past wickedness, I am afraid to live any longer, and I am weary of all the trials of this exile.

Divine Consolations Granted Contemplatives

There is nothing surprising in the fact that those who have contemplated some of the perfections of God should desire to behold them in all their glory and to dwell in that heavenly abode where their souls will be filled with them. As a consequence, such persons long to quit this earth, where they encounter so many obstacles, and to enter upon the enjoyment of their supreme good, and yearn for their dwelling in the Father's house where the Sun of Justice will never set. How dull everything must appear to them after such a favor! It is a cause of wonder to me how they can even bear to live. Those who have begun to taste divine consolations and who have received the pledges of the heavenly realm can find no contentment here on earth. It they remain here, it is not because they desire to do so, but because of the will of their King.

The Vicissitudes of Life

How different that life of heaven must be from life on earth! In heaven, no one longs for death! And how differently the human will fulfills the will of God in heaven! God wills that we love truth, but here we love falsehood. He wills that we strive only for what is eternal, and we seek what is fleeting. He wills that we aspire to the noble and sublime, and we seek what is base and earthly. He wills that we should love security, and we love what is uncertain.

Requesting Great Favors

What folly it is to do anything else but pray to God to deliver us forever from such dangers and to free us from all evil! Even though our desire for this grace is far from perfect, let us request it with importunity. What does it cost us to ask so great a favor, since we address our prayer to the omnipotent God? It would be an insult indeed to ask a powerful emperor for only a farthing. But that we may succeed the better in our petitions, let us leave the choice of gifts to him, for we have already surrendered our wills into his hands. May his name be forever blessed in heaven and on earth, and may his will be always fulfilled in me!

Sublimity of Vocal Prayer

Now you see how vocal prayer can be perfect. It consists in considering and realizing who he is from whom we ask this petition, who we are who petition, and what it is we really seek. Do not be disheartened, then, if you are told to limit yourself to vocal prayer. Reread attentively what I have written here, and if you do not understand what has been said about prayer, ask our Lord to enlighten you. Pray vocally; no one can hinder you. Nor is there anyone who can oblige you to recite the Our Father in haste, and without reflecting on what you are saying. Pay no heed to anyone who would influence or counsel you to pray thoughtlessly. You may be sure that such a one is a false prophet. Remember, too, that in these perilous times, we ought not to believe the first comer. Undoubtedly, you have nothing to fear from those who are counseling you at the present time, but as to what may happen in the future, we cannot say.

I had hoped to speak to you, too, about the recitation of the Hail Mary. However, I have discoursed so much on the Our Father, that I now forego that plan. As for that matter, if we understand how we ought to recite the Our Father perfectly, we shall know how to recite all other vocal prayers.

The Way of Perfection

See how our Lord has assisted me in this work. He has taught both you and me the way of perfection that I began to explain. He has made me understand what great things we request when we recite this prayer of the Gospel. May he be blessed forever and ever!

The Sublime Mysteries of the Our Father

I assure you that I never dreamed this prayer contained such deep secrets. You will have noticed that it sums up the entire spiritual life, from its first beginning to that point where the soul is lost entirely in God, and where he refreshes it at the Font of Living Water, which is found, as I told you, at the summit of the way of perfection.

Our Lord has willed to show us what consoling truths this prayer contains. It is extremely profitable for those persons who cannot read. If they were to understand it well, they would find much instruction and consolation therein. Though all our books were taken from us, no one could deprive us of this one which has come to us from the very lips of him who is Truth and who cannot deceive. Moreover, since we repeat the Our Father so often during the day, let us find joy in reciting it.

Humility and the Other Virtues

Finally, let the example of our glorious Master in humble prayer teach us humility. Let us likewise learn from him all the other virtues of which we have spoken. Ask him to pardon my boldness in treating of such sublime subjects. Our Sovereign Master well knew that, unless he taught me what to say, I should be unequal to this task. Thank him then for everything. If he has deigned to assist me, it was undoubtedly because of the humility you manifested in requesting this writing, and in condescending to be taught by so miserable a creature as I am.

Teachings on Prayer

It seems that he does not wish me to continue, despite my desire to do so, though truthfully, I do not know what I could add. It is he who has taught you the way of perfection. In another book (St. Teresa's *Autobiography,* chapters 10 to 24), I have indicated what you are to do once you have reached the Fountain of Living Water, what the soul experiences there, how God satiates the soul, how he deprives it of the desire for all earthly things, and how he helps it to grow in his service. These considerations will be helpful for the souls elevated to this state, and will enlighten them considerably. Try to get this book. At present, it is in the possession of Father Dominic Bañez, to whom also I shall entrust this volume. If he considers it useful for your souls, and gives it to you to read, I shall be happy at the thought of the consolation you will derive from it. But if he decides that it is not to be read by anyone, be kind enough to accept my good intentions. At least, I have done everything possible to comply with your request.

Consolations Derived From Study of the Mysteries of God

I consider myself well rewarded for the effort expended in composing this. But beyond the mere writing, I have done nothing; for assuredly I have not had to labor over what I was to say. I have derived the greatest consolation from the understanding of the secret mysteries our Lord made known to me in this prayer of his Gospel. May he be blessed and praised forever! From him comes all the good ever found in our words, thoughts, and deeds! Amen.

Teresa of Avila (1515–1582) was a contemplative nun, religious reformer, spiritual writer, and gifted poet who lived during a period of reform and bitter religious rivalry in Western Europe.

During his lifetime, **William J. Doheny, C.S.C.**, (1898–1982) was Dean of the Notre Dame Law School, Assistant Superior of the Congregation of Holy Cross, and Advocate and Procurator of the Roman Rota. This book is one of many that he personally published and distributed to religious and lay readers to foster the knowledge and practice of prayer.